SURGE

來到泥丸宮

Tai Chi
SURGE

Radical ZMQ Energetics

by Scott Meredith

Illustrated by Jeremy Ray

See Otter Books

Published by See Otter Books

ISBN: 978-1-5061-1955-7

Typesetting services by BOOKOW.COM

Dedication

To the memory of the master jeweler,

WANG ZONGYUE
王宗岳

who cut, polished, and set Tai Chi –
the mysteriously radiant gem.

* * *

To the greatest Tai Chi master
of his generation,

BENJAMIN PANG JENG LO
羅邦楨

who is in no way responsible
for any part of this wild book.

Notes

All translations from the Chinese and Japanese are the original copyrighted work of the author unless otherwise explicitly sourced.

Most Chinese characters are traditional, with occasional variation including adoption of simplified characters, based on common usage, personal preference, and accepted historical precedent in names, among other criteria.

Most Chinese transliterations are Pinyin, with occasional variation including adoption of Wade-Giles and other variants, based on common usage, personal preference, and accepted historical precedent in names, among other criteria.

Disclaimer

All practices, processes, and methods described in this book are provided for entertainment purposes only. All martial arts practices including Tai Chi entail risks including, but not limited to, permanent disability and death.

Never engage in any physical practice except under the oversight of currently certified and licensed health care professionals.

Do not attempt anything described in this book without the full knowledge, consent, and personal supervision of a qualified, currently licensed physician or other qualified health care professional. This book may not be used to diagnose or treat any medical condition.

The publisher and author are not responsible for any specific health or allergy needs that may require medical supervision and are not liable for any damages or negative consequences from any treatment, action, application or preparation, to any person reading or following the information in this book.

The author and publisher make no representations or warranties of any kind and assume no liabilities of any kind with respect to the accuracy or completeness of the contents and specifically disclaim any implied warranties of merchantability or fitness of use for a particular purpose.

Neither the author nor the publisher shall be held liable or responsible to any person or entity with respect to any loss or incidental or consequential damages caused, or alleged to have been caused, directly or indirectly, by the information or programs contained herein.

Protect yourself at all times.

CONTENTS

Preface   1

Fable   4

Introduction   5

Energy Substrate   14

Tai Chi Structure Principles   17

A Further Note on Relaxation   19

The Cat-Step Protocol   22
Cat-Step SOLE 27
Cat-Step HEEL 27
Cat-Step REAR 28
Cat-Step PARTIAL 28

Cat-Step Imagery   29

Cat-Step: Left Wardoff Example   32

The Counter-Sink Protocol   49

Counter-Sink: Single Whip Example   57

Duration   65

How to Work It   66

Barriers, Hang-Ups, Impediments   69

Pose Notes   **72**
    Section 1 75
    Section 2 98

Bread Sandwich Tai Chi   **119**

Advanced Work   **121**
    Cat-Step Protocol/CYCLING: 121
    Counter-Sink Protocol/PACKING: 122
    Cestus Protocol/EDGING: 125
    Counter-Sink Protocol/PINNING: 127
    Cat-Step Protocol/GAPPING: 130
    WU BI ZHUANG (無臂樁) Armless Standing 131
    Zhang Zhuang/PINNED 133
    Counter-Sink Protocol/SUPER SURGE: 136

Refund Policy   **138**

The Big Picture   **144**

Bibliography   **147**

PREFACE

This book accompanies the planned DVD: *Tai Chi GROUND Radical ZMQ Energetics*. I say 'planned' because, as of this writing in early 2015, the DVD hasn't been finalized.

Even for small scale productions like mine, there are lots of hassles in making a DVD that don't apply to books. The shooting, editing, composing footage with text, music, graphics, effects, main and sub -menus, etc., is very time-consuming. Then, whereas the publisher takes about 48 *hours* to approve and list a new book title, that same publisher takes four *months* to inspect and approve a DVD (with numerous back-and-forth emails dealing with little compression quibbles and audio issues and whatnot all along the way). That's one reason I'm providing this material in print, as a way to get these ideas and practices out the door quickly to those who may care to try them.

I can also explain things in more depth here. In the visual DVD format, talk is boring. The *Tai Chi Ground* film is mainly oriented to teaching the internal energy practices, or *intensifiers*, in the context of a forensically detailed, minute deconstruction of every single pose and transition in the Zheng Manqing 37-move simplified Tai Chi form. Though it's said to consist of 37 postures, when you add up all the main poses, the duplicated poses, plus some variations that I like to teach, as well as all the transitions between poses, you end up with well over 60 moves – many of which contain three or more sub-gestures.

That's lot of talking, just to do justice to the plain mechanics and structural aspects. *Arm here leg there* stuff. Boring to listen to! Yet only a DVD can do justice to the external mechanics and movements. However, what I want to put out isn't mainly the mechanics and structures; rather it's the *nei gong* or internal substrate of this amazing system. And that's going to need more talk than any DVD watcher could possibly tolerate. Readers, on the other hand, can deal with a lot of hot air and long-winded discourse. That's good because it's gotta be more *tell* than *show*.

This book differs from my earlier work as follows: In *Juice*, I wanted to break out of the physicalized conception of Tai Chi that has become dominant, across all styles and flavors. So although the discussion there uses the ZMQ37 as a touchstone, it shoots for style -neutrality and deals with the underlying energetic foundations of Tai Chi.

In *Peng*, I zoomed in on core elements of the ZMQ approach, but the method there is mainly for people who are unable for whatever reason to learn or consistently practice the full ZMQ37 method. The methods in the *Peng* book are snippets that help you to get some of the essence of this incredible energetic system, but the training there is only a distillate and subset of what's possible. In this book, I show the full depth of the ZMQ37 system, in detail, with the internal conditioning explicitly integrated with the details of postures and transitions.

JUICE is a love letter, *PENG* is a travel guide, *SURGE* is the owner's manual. The deep point of all three books is identical. The overall idea is that Tai Chi is a miracle method of internal development. But to experience that, you must shed the material blinders that keep you tunnel-visioned on physical *mechanics* and performance *theatrics*.

इतीन्द्रियाणि सन्त्यज्य स्वस्थः स्वात्मनि वर्तते

Marvel that once, you identified with
Only the surface of this ocean.

Now, embrace the tides, depths, undersea mountains,
Out to the farthest shore.

- Sutra of the *Vijnana Bhairava Tantra*

FABLE

Drona ordered the princes, one by one, to aim their arrows from a hundred yards distance at the eye of a carved and painted wooden parrot, placed on the highest branch of a tall jamun tree growing in the Acharya's own garden.

'What do you see?' he asked them.

Yudhishtira said, 'I see a parrot.'

'Don't waste your arrow. Step back.'

Duryodhana, determined to outshine Yudhishtira, said, 'I see a carved parrot on a high tree branch.'

'Don't waste your arrow. Step back.'

Bhima, anxious to outdo Duryodhana, said, 'I see a carved parrot on a high tree branch under a cloudy sky.'

'Don't waste your arrow. Step back.'

Arjuna said, 'I see an eye.'

'You may shoot', said Drona. The arrow pierced straight through the mark.

- Mahabharata

INTRODUCTION

What the bleep *is* Tai Chi anyway? Dance? Fight? Health and beauty aid? New Age fantasy? Or what?

Figure 1: What is Tai Chi? Dance? Fight? Therapy? New Age fantasy?

It *can* serve all those ends. For purposes of this book, it will seem that I'm narrowing the entrance ramp - but work it as I explain and you'll find yourself out on the freeway. The purpose here is one thing: *develop your internal energy.* To the point that you can feel it. To the point that it practically *blows you totally away.* That's the only goal here. Once you have that going, you can revisit all the other stuff on your own.

All that other stuff (dance, fight, health, whatever) may follow on from this energetic opening, depending on your attributes, interests, and talents. But those things are beyond the scope of this book. This book is Tai Chi as 內功 (*nei gong*; inner work), plain and simple. That means learning to experience, control, and amplify the surge of power from your *feet* through your *body* to your *hands*.

Four basic concepts undergird this phenomenal practice. They are:

- Grounding
- Relaxation
- Extension
- Mindfulness

Other types of *qi gong* and *nei gong* cover bits and pieces of these, but only Zheng Manqing Tai Chi - the Grand Ultimate Fist - puts it all together optimally and most powerfully.

I feel most people who enter the Tai Chi store aren't really getting what they came in for. Maybe that's just me being an arrogant prick. But even an arrogant prick can be right sometimes. It astonishes me that people who've practiced for years have internal energy experience (if their own testimony can be relied on), comparable to dipping one toe in a parking lot rain puddle, while Oahu's north shore winter surf thunders on the beach just beyond.

They settle for too little, relative to what's possible. The Tai Chi Classics are chock full of open, brazen, unembarrassed assertions about pure internal energy, yet after years of practice, we end up settling for outcomes like 'feeling calmer' or 'having better balance'. Bleh! Boring. If *that's* all it was, I wouldn't bother with it.

Part of the problem is the ZMQ37 simplified Tai Chi form. ZMQ stands for Zheng Man Qing, the master of Five Excellences, the genius who somehow cooked up this 37-pose method in the early/mid 20th century, from bits and pieces of internal practices scattered around Eastern China. Professor Zheng is all over the web and YouTube so don't worry - I'm not going to get into all the tedious history and backchat on it.

His form of Tai Chi was one of the first to gain an international toehold outside the Chinese community. It's been around so long we take it for granted. We now want something fresher and more exciting. Paradoxically, one way something can seem fresher is if it can claim an older or more mysterious pedigree. So some styles have seen their stock rise on the basis of historical pedigree and political prestige.

Another factor that has counted against the ZMQ style is how plain-Jane it *looks*. It doesn't make for exciting demos. We don't sit as low as Style X, we don't wiffle our hands in the scary fashion of Style Y, we don't stomp or jump like Style Z. We rarely even wear silk pajamas. It's just no fun to the childlike *spectator* mind. It doesn't delight the eye and ear.

Finally, *mea culpa*, I must admit that we ZMQ-ster's haven't exactly burned up the Octagon or smeared the cage with the blood of our vanquished martial arts opponents. Apart from a few kickass exceptions, ZMQ as the training basis of a serious fight game is a hard sell.

I understand all these factors. Yet... as a person who has intensively trained an uncountable number of body work, breath work, and energy work systems intensively for more than forty years, I still chauvinistically insist that ZMQ Tai Chi is a thing of peerless genius.

Even I don't quite understand what little nuance or touch makes the ZMQ37 so special. It simply has that inexplicable *x-factor* of greatness.

This book answers the perennial question of how to work the ZMQ form to its full potential as the greatest extended Nei Gong method ever created. Although the ZMQ37 appears painted over as an ordinary wave-your-arms Tai Chi set, and is normally toe-tagged (with a yawn) as such, in fact it is very far being merely that, and I'm going to show why.

It seems impossible that such a simple, accessible program can be all *that* great. Especially because the ZMQ37 is essentially structural and formulaic, rather than mystically Daoist, in look and feel. Yet neither is it the fashionable materialist revisionism, which is inordinately hung up on physiological stuff like fascia, bones, and joint vectors. How can such a workaday system generate such outlandish internal effects? Even I am at a loss to say.

My DVD *Tai Chi GROUND Radical ZMQ Energetics* presents every pose and every transition of the ZMQ37 form, showing and describing every key point of intensification and reinforcement of the *peng* energy flow. I'll describe *peng* energy more explicitly further on, but for now think of it as a soft wave of palpable power that emanates from your feet, and surges through your legs and torso, before culminating in a burst at your fingertips.

I went deeply into the energy theory in my earlier books, *JUICE Radical Taiji Energetics* and *Tai Chi PENG Root Power Rising*. So though I'll cover some of that, if you're curious about energy theory I'd like to refer you to those works, and save space here to focus on the *how* of it, more than the *why* or the *what*.

To my knowledge the intensifier methods described in the DVD and this book have never been explicitly taught - neither by me nor anybody else – but they are fully implied by the Tai Chi classics and directly inferable from there. This is essentially the application and extension of key ideas in the *Peng* book to the ZMQ37 form *as a whole*. It's the *Peng* book raised to the 10th power.

My *Peng* book was geared to illustrating the absolute minimality of internal energy practice. Minimal in terms of space, learning time, practice time, complexity, etc. - every kind of overhead cut to the bone. But here, I'm going to assume that you know or are learning the ZMQ37 form from some other resource. This book is meant to be a private supplement to that learning.

There are three potential audiences for this book:

1. **Practitioners and learners of ZMQ37:** This is the core audience because they have the necessary toolkit in hand. While I de-emphasize structure for it's own sake or for performance aesthetics, certain postural basics are essential. Those take time to sink in. It isn't possible to learn the ZMQ37 mechanics thoroughly and correctly from any book or DVD, certainly not mine. So people who already have a teacher can benefit most, from knowing the pre-requisites. At the same time, having an established practice under a teacher can be a hindrance in some cases, because it can make students afraid to experiment and trust their own reactions.

2. **Practitioners and learners of other Tai Chi styles:** This is an interesting group because they will face the challenge, if they choose to accept it, of finding a way to apply the ideas here to a framework that may slightly "resist" their efforts. The methods here are based on the ZMQ37 property that *your form never*

fights you. What I mean is, your form should not include any element that is less than fully relaxed, less than optimal for relaxation. That means no straight or locked arms or legs, no leaning, no sharply bent wrists, no heavy stepping, no forceful whiplashing of limbs, no extraneous hand shaking in the name of *fajing* theatrics – and a lot of other requirements. Another option for these people is to switch on over to ZMQ37.

3. **Total Tai Chi newbies**: These people will either have to work entirely within the restricted (yet powerful) 7-pose framework of the *Peng* book (to which the ideas here can be applied with some imagination on your part) or else find a ZMQ37 teacher. You won't be able to learn the full ZMQ form, starting at zero, from either my DVD or this book. But for those who want to stick with the reduced PENG version of seven basic poses, this book will give you more practice ideas as feedstock.

Ten weeks of consistent and careful practice of this book's intensified mode will yield greater results in **grounding, relaxation, extension** and **mental control** of the *peng* energy than up to ten years of practicing the postures and sequence outside this intensified framework.

REPETITION?

Most assuredly there will be a kind of repetition to it. That's what training with a Master mostly is (I don't mean I'm a Master, I mean I'm trying to give your practice a small taste of the feeling produced by sessions with my teacher). My very earliest teacher Robert Smith often quoted this to us: *In all spiritual disciplines, everything of importance is contained in the first lesson.* Once I finally found a true Master, my eventual real teacher, I learned the depth of that wisdom. So there's repetition like a constant rhythm, but also melodic variation, because each pose is subtly different.

The key concept here is **no move left behind**, meaning that every pose, step, transition and gesture should generate a palpable, fully tangible energetic engagement and strengthening. I never form a pose mechanically just for the sake of getting it done, or overall feeling good. You should exploit the hell out of every moment and movement of your precious practice time.

Take the same mentality toward your practice time as the American Indians had to a bison they hunted down. They made full use of every piece, the meat, the hide, the organs, the bones, and the tail whisk – all of him! In this book I'll apply that kind of thinking to the form, so that no motion is left energetically unengaged. Never think of your form time as a *practice* session. It should always be an *experience* session.

POSTURE PERFECTION?

The ZMQ37 functions as a launch pad for the raw, uncut *peng* power SURGE. It's not a beauty contest or fashion show.

You can't learn the ZMQ37 form from this book. As for film, only two people on earth have ever performed the ZMQ postures *perfectly* in terms of shape and kinetics (Zheng Manqing and Benjamin Lo). For truly mastering the mechanics, you'll need to get hold of my teacher's video and you'll also have to spend hours stepping frame -by-frame through Professor Zheng's films.

That, or get a good teacher. But even a good teacher must necessarily devote most of class time to working on mechanics and structure. They rarely have time to delve into the internal power aspects. They're more worried about whether you may be leaning this way or that, or losing your balance on the kicks, or damaging your knee with mis-alignment – practical stuff. I have the freedom here to talk more cosmically.

That said, this book covers the mechanics well enough to get you started on applying the intensified *nei gong* protocols to your practice. That will open up the inner content of the set.

STAGES

(1) In the first month of practicing as directed in this book, you'll begin to feel an amazing increase in your leg strength. It's a physical thing, based on the slow stepping and the low sitting, and it feels great.

(2) In the second month of practicing as directed here, you'll begin to experience a loosening and relaxation of many parts of your body. This is partly done by consciously noticing tension you hadn't known was present. The careful stepping makes you aware of unconscious tension. Some of the big steps are almost impossible if you retain even a trace of unnecessary muscular engagement. There will also be a lessening of tension as you learn to feel and augment the energy flow along the entire track of feet to fingers, not just concentrating energy in one point, area, or bounded channel as is often done in meditation and other martial arts.

(3) In month three, you'll start feeling the energy flow from the soles of your feet to the inner surface of your hands. You'll be amazed. Even if you've felt little buzzes and tingles in previous energy work, this is an order of magnitude beyond.

(4) By month four, I hope you'll be hooked on this practice for life and take the internal power to infinity and beyond. Let's redeem the name of this venerable martial art.

METHOD

Relaxation - Grounding - Extension - Mindfulness

Those 4 attributes are what differentiate Tai Chi from garden variety Qi Gong.

I'm going to introduce two training methods for these attributes which can be intimately welded into your daily form practice and which will hugely amplify and expedite your internal development. The ZMQ form is a gem beyond price, but without these two principles explicitly worked by you on every pose and transition, the form will always remain just a diamond in the rough.

Figure 2: Practicing Tai Chi without explicit attention to the internal energy is like owning a Lamborghini without any tires.

There are two main internal training protocols, the Cat-Step and the Counter-Sink. These are solidly rooted in the Tai Chi Classics, so you don't need to be afraid of them or fret that your teacher would be scandalized if s/he found out you're reading this. But I'm going to break them down into more specific detail than the Classics do, to use them for internal energy generation.

ENERGY SUBSTRATE

I covered a lot on the energy hotspots and power tracks of the body in earlier books. While this book builds on the earlier concepts, it's centered on introducing practical, new(ish) ZMQ-based training methods. So here I'm only going to repeat the most bare-bones introduction to the framework, a minor and lesser-known Tai Chi Classic of energy movement.

There are small differences of emphasis in this Classic relative to my own way of experiencing and teaching, but don't sweat that because overall, this guy *pretty well nailed it*. The relevant lines are these:

神氣運行歌

Verses on Energy Transmission

氣如長江水, 滔滔向東流

Qi power is like the eastward-surging Yangzi River torrent

來自湧泉穴, 路經脊背過

Starting at the feet, from the sole's central point, rising up through the spinal channel

來到泥丸宮, 回到印堂闕

Continuing upward to the niwan center, then lowering into the brow point

心意將氣領, 從不稍離別

The mind leads the qi, the two never diverging even slightly

譬如右拳舉, 意氣到手腋

Let's say the right hand prepares to strike - the mind directs the qi to the armpit

隨勁意氣到, 覺之在肘窩

The mind then manifests the qi as palpable internal power through the crook of the elbow

順勢一反拳, 意氣到內關穴

As the hand turns upward, the mind guides the qi power through the inner wrist

右拳前按出, 掌心微突越

When the right hand pushes out, the palm center bulges slightly

氣經掌陰面, 直到五指尖

The qi energy, passing across the surface of the inner hand, directly charges the five fingers

There's more but what's above is all that matters for this book. He has brilliantly laid out the basics. But within this general framework, the energy can manifest in your personal experience with surprising variety. The ZMQ37 Tai Chi will trigger every possible energy manifestation.

Just as matter exists in different modes – solid, liquid, vapor, plasma – so will your energy experience freak you out with its power, intensity, and variety. Even within a single manifestation category there are all the variations familiar from the natural elements. For example, when you experience the energy as a 'liquid' or water, it still has the tremendous range of water's mercurial nature – e.g. static density as a lake; deep sluicing as a broad river; ferocious turbulence like whitewater rapids; implacable saturation like the creep of a night tide; incessant battering like coastal waves; or the long, slow surging of blue-water ocean swells.

The internal energy work as developed through the ZMQ37 form is tied with (and probably ultimately exceeds) sex as the most pleasurable and fascinating thing you can experience in a human body. So there's your *what*. For more on all that, I refer you to *Juice: Radical Tai Chi Energetics.* The remainder of this book deals with *how*.

TAI CHI STRUCTURE PRINCIPLES

1. **Relax:** No unnecessary tension in your body, but don't collapse.

2. **Body Upright:** Don't lean in any direction, unless the pose calls for it.

3. **Beautiful Lady's Hand:** Your wrist is kept straight, flat and extended at all times.

4. **Separate Weight:** In every pose, one leg will have greater weight than the other. Only at the start and finish is the pose 50-50 weighted.

5. **Turn Waist:** All physical movement is initiated from the waist, not your arms. Additionally, you 'turn' your waist straight to the direction of the pose vector (South, East, etc.), which is the line of your sight and your nose. You never cant the waist diagonally sideways.

Front Weighted Stance: 70/30

The most common lower body configuration in the form is the front-weighted 70/30 stance. 70% of your body weight is supported by the front leg, and 30% to the rear. If you have read my book *Peng*, you may understand that you could also use 80/20 as your base figure here. Either way is fine.

Here are some additional structural considerations for this important stance:

1. **Front Knee** always directly above toe (protect your knees)

2. **Waist** facing front, straight along the pose's main vector

3. **Hip Joint** bent so that the angle at the inguinal crease of the 70% weighted front leg is no more open than 90 degrees

4. **Rear Foot** flat at 45 degrees, do not let the outer edge of the foot roll upward. Your rear knee relaxes at a natural angle

The side-to-side distance of your feet would be shoulder-width if you withdrew the front foot straight back in a line to place alongside the rear foot. The front-to-back distance is no more than you could "undo'. To check the 'undo' requirement in a front-weighted stance, you sit *back* entirely, placing all body weight into your rear leg. Then you should be able to comfortably raise your *front* foot, *in situ* without changing its placement, with no loss of balance, wobbling, compensation, distortion, or leaning. If this cannot be done, you've taken too long a front-to-back foot placement in the 70/30 pose.

A Further Note on Relaxation

If you want to go east, don't go west.

- Ramakrishna

I won't be able to keep on harping every other paragraph about *relaxation* being the alpha and omega of the entire ZMQ37 game. But I would if I could.

Here's the thing. Some people actually try to *justify* the deliberate use of tension in Tai Chi and other internal methods. I'm perfectly well aware that even the sublimely engineered ZMQ37 poses require some muscle to hold, as does merely standing up against gravity. Further, I'm well aware that our hearts and kidneys etc. are muscular pumps.

Does anybody not know those things? Isn't all of that obvious? Where do these observations *get* us? I'm a practical person. I focus on one thing: *what do you **do** in your internal training?* It's a practical point because we don't have much time on this earth and in these bodies.

If you tell me that the poses require some little bit of tension to hold, what new have you told me? Isn't that like: DOH! That isn't the question. And the question isn't theoretical either, so forget about kidneys and heart pumping and gravity and all that.

The question is *practical*, as follows:

Beyond the obvious minimum strength needed to stand in the ZMQ37 poses and train them correctly, is there any place whatsoever for **any additional, conscious application of muscular tension,** *as an aspect of the internal training regimen, beyond the minimum needed to hold and perform those poses correctly?*

Well - *is there?* That's the only **practical** question!

If you start talking about how a bit of muscle is needed to hold the poses (obviously!) or about your heart and kidneys, or about gravity or about various exotic complex traditional training regimens you may have heard of or learned that make use of tension, you are getting away from the point. You are creating a subtle justification that your subconscious mind (which *loves* the feeling of pseudo-power that muscle tension confers) will use to justify the injection of even more unconscious tension than you have already.

It's a *practical* point. Not a theoretical discussion!

If you want to experience the maximum of Tai Chi internal power, reduce all tension in your poses to an absolute minimum.

Why is that a big Jesuitical debate? Just do that.

If you don't believe me, will you take the words of three generations of off-the-charts Yang system masters? Tell me if any part of the following three quotations seems ambiguous:

In practicing T'ai Chi Ch'uan the whole body relaxes. Don't let even one ounce of tension linger in the blood vessels, bones, and ligaments to cramp yourself up.

- Yang Chengfu

You must be completely relaxed, only then can you respond spontaneously and unknowably to every condition. You must be as relaxed as a bag of bones, only this can properly be called relaxation. Never forget that you'll never be able to issue energy as long as you cling to any residual tension whatsoever.

- Li Yaxuan

T'ai Chi Ch'uan as an art of self-defense must completely spurn muscular force.

- Zheng Manqing

The Cat-Step Protocol

The basic idea of the Cat-Step Protocol (CSP) is nothing new. Every beginning Tai Chi student is familiar with possibly the most famous line in all the Tai Chi classic writings:

邁步如貓行

mài bù rú māo xíng

Step like a cat.

Some Tai Chi students believe that as long as they're trying, *most* of the time, when they *remember* it, to step kind of softly and lightly and without too much of a big elephantine THUMP as they place their foot down into the next pose, they're good to go. But in fact, there's a much greater depth to, and harvest from, this idea than most Tai Chi people ever get near.

Many Tai Chi students never even attempt the Cat-Step at all, in even rudimentary form. And those who have heard of it and try to step in the spirit of it, are sometimes lacking the precise technical details that make the Cat-Step SURGE possible.

I'm going to get really anal on this and break it down minutely to show all its variations. But before I geek on over to the mechanics, I want to lay out the main point of it all. The *idea* of Cat-Step sounds kind of cool, so I think most of us accept that it's a nice-sounding, naturalistic kind of thing and we let it go at that. But in fact, it's an extremely technical method that has a specific and amazing energetic effect.

When you do the Cat-Step protocol correctly and consistently, you will begin to feel what I call the Cat-Step SURGE. This is a strong wave of soft *peng* energy, blasting quickly upward from both feet, through your torso and back, lightly ascending through your head and then powering through your arms to your hands. It's a distinct sensation – just as "real" as anything else you can experience such as pain, cold, heat, orgasm, itchiness, or a sneeze. But it's way more intense, powerful and pleasurable than (most) of the things on that list.

Readers familiar with my book *Tai Chi Peng* will recognize that the CSP is the extension of the in-place foot-weighting mechanism (Free, Zero, Rest, Relax, and Surge described for the Cloud Hands drill in that book), to the entire ZMQ37 form. The 7 poses of the *Peng* book were selected for precision work with the three basic concepts of Cat-Step weighting. FREE (called RAISED in the present book) is exemplified in the Golden Rooster and Separate Leg poses. TOUCH (called ZERO in this book) and REST are exemplified for the front foot in Raise Hands and Repulse Monkey poses, while REST is exemplified for the rear foot with the Peng, Single Whip, and Weaving Lady poses (20% rear leg weight is the REST condition).

To apply the system to the ZMQ form as a whole, we stipulate that every time we change the Position, Angle, or Weighting (PAW) of either foot, we will train the Cat-Step stages and feel the SURGE. Change of *position* means re-situating the foot in a different place on the floor. Change of *angle* means rotation of the foot, either on the big toe or front shoe or else on the heel. Change of *weighting* deals with degrees of body weight placed on a given foot at a given point in a transition. The CSP can be integrated with all these normal ZMQ stepping dynamics.

The stages are as follows:

1. RAISE: This is easy; you only need to maintain a gap, just a few centimeters, between your foot and the floor. (This was called FREE in the *Peng* book). This is how every Cat-Step begins. You try to relax your foot and your ankle as much as possible before starting to lower. Feel that your foot is like the soft hairs of a Chinese calligraphy brush, and your lower leg is the brush handle.

2. TOUCH: There are some variations as to which part of the foot touches down first, to be covered below. But the basic idea here is the same for all variations: you are only touching – it's pure contact, without any weight applied from your foot, leg, or body, and without accepting any support from the floor (this was called ZERO in the *Peng* book). It's like touching a light switch on the wall – you don't apply any body weight to it, only contact alone. You try to relax your leg as much as possible (same as *always* with *everything* in Tai Chi) but despite your best efforts you'll find that a bit of muscular engagement is needed in the leg and the hip area to keep any weight from sinking into the floor. So just feel whatever bit of tension comes up in this phase, as that is one purpose of all this: *becoming aware*. I need to emphasize the importance of this TOUCH stage. If you rush through this, if you don't feel it explicitly for at least a second or two at every Cat-Step, you won't get much of a SURGE in the final stage, below. This TOUCH stage, where your foot has merely the barest contact with the floor without any weight but without losing that contact, is both physically difficult and more importantly, a mental challenge. It seems

like it's no big deal, so over time you'll find yourself eliding this stage, kind of sliding past it, mushing it together between preceding RAISE and following REST (or even LOAD). But if you do that, you've lost the whole point and probably won't experience a strong (if any) Cat-Step SURGE. It's precisely the mental difficulty of calibrating that touch-without-weight condition that nails your *mind* into the stepping foot and primes the compressed energy flood that you'll experience a moment later as the SURGE rising through the whole body. Remember *energy follows mind.* So work with every one of these Cat-Step stages distinctly and precisely. Don't start eliding things because you think you know what this is. It's beyond what you may think right now. Doing the ZMQ with the Cat-Step (as defined here, not as you may have thought you knew it) and the Counter-Sink will soon show you why I constantly bleat that the workaday, unsexy plain-Jane ZMQ Tai Chi form is the greatest *nei gong* method ever.

3. REST: There are variations in the areas of the foot involved, but the idea is the same across all variants. This can be a little hard for some people to wrap their head around: you allow the floor to support *the weight of your leg alone.* So in a way, it's beginning to load some weight, yet of a special type. In the *Peng* book, I mentioned research showing that a single leg comprises about 20% of total body weight. That's all it should be here. Visually it appears identical to the previous TOUCH phase, but if you play a bit you'll feel it's very different. In this phase, you can relax whatever scintilla of tension was needed in the TOUCH phase to keep any weight off the floor. Now since you're allowing the floor to support your leg, you can truly relax all the previously engaged muscles.

4. RELAX: When you're sure you have the leg's weight, and *only* the leg's weight, supported by the floor, try one more time to

truly relax everything in the leg. Foot, ankle, calf, knee, thigh, and butt – everything.

5. SURGE: As you complete your final check in the RELAX stage, you'll suddenly feel the Cat-Step SURGE. It is a wave of soft *peng* energy that zips up your legs, through your *dantian*, sacrum, torso and back, lightly through your neck, head, and fore-head, then instantly down through your arms to fingers. This SURGE is the payoff and ultimate point of the whole Cat-Step method. The SURGE happens pretty quickly, maybe a half second or so from feet to fingers, maybe a full second. This is not an abstraction, a word, a concept, a visualization, an idea, a long term goal, a translation of ancient Chinese philosophy, a fuzzy, vague term for what you think I'm *really* trying to say if I weren't so scientifically ignorant (such as fascia tissue or bio-whatever), nor is it a marketing buzz phrase or anything else. It's an internal energy training reality that you can play with now that you've been taught how to generate it.

6. LOAD: After you've experienced the Cat-Step SURGE - on every change of PAW in the transition - *then and only then* you may begin to load actual body weight (beyond the leg's own weight as above) onto the given leg. As you begin to LOAD the weight, mentally flash your awareness down to the bottom of the sole of your LOAD-ing foot, right where the whole shoe bottom is flush against the floor, just for an instant as your LOAD begins. Doing this will strengthen your entire body's energy over time.

There are four main stepping modes in the ZMQ form: SOLE, HEEL, REAR and PARTIAL. We apply the CSP to all of these, as follows:

Cat-Step SOLE

RAISED: *Foot is raised above floor, no contact.*

TOUCH: *Flat sole touches, no weight at all.*

REST: *Flat sole touches, relax leg muscles so floor supports leg's weight only. Body weight in rear leg.*

RELAX: *Loosen every muscle of the leg.*

SURGE

LOAD: *Transfer weight onto the leg.*

Cat-Step HEEL

RAISED: *Foot is raised above floor, no contact.*

TOUCH: *Heel touches, no weight at all.*

REST 1: *Heel touches, floor supports leg's weight only.*

REST 2: *Entire sole touches, floor supports leg's weight only. Body weight in rear leg.*

RELAX: *Loosen every muscle of the leg.*

SURGE

LOAD: *Transfer weight onto the leg.*

Cat-Step REAR

RAISED: *Foot is raised above floor, no contact.*

TOUCH: *Big toe part of shoe touches floor, no weight.*

REST 1: *Big toe part of shoe touches floor, floor supports leg weight only.*

REST 2: *Whole sole touches, floor supports leg weight only. Body weight in front leg.*

RELAX: *Loosen every muscle of the leg.*

SURGE

LOAD: *Transfer weight onto the leg.*

Cat-Step PARTIAL

RAISED: *Foot is raised above floor, no contact.*

TOUCH: *Heel or big toe touches, no weight.*

REST: *Floor supports leg's weight only. Body weight in rear leg.*

RELAX: *Loosen every muscle of the leg.*

SURGE

(Note that PARTIAL mode usually ends with another RAISE of the same foot, rather than a LOAD of weight onto it.)

Cat-Step Imagery

I'm going to push this whole *cat* metaphor even farther now. I'm not doing this merely to align myself more tightly with the Tai Chi classics, or for the sake of hearing my own voice. This kind of imagery helps you to *feel this stuff for real*, for yourself.

Once you've felt that SURGE a few times, even the highly attenuated version that you'll get in the early stages, you'll be launched, hooked, addicted. You'll take off on your own and you won't need this book. My job is nothing more than getting you over the starting line. So let's squeeze this cat imagery for all it's worth.

The Cat-Step directive suggests a certain delicacy of step and paw placement, combined with a relaxed athletic power in the walk. That's the usual interpretation, and it's true and useful. But I'm going to get into it more deeply.

The big cats, especially lions, often rest with their paws turned sideways or upward, as shown in the figures overleaf. That allows for a close-up view of the structure of the paw, with *tufts* of fur surrounding large, soft *pads*. We can use these images to greatly intensify our practice.

When you do the TOUCH phase of any Cat-Step, imagine that what's in physical contact with the floor are those short and soft *tufts* of fur in the paw (your foot when you do Tai Chi). Imagine how sensitive and relaxed your foot would have to be to feel the barest brush of those tufts on the floor. Just barely contacting, without any weight

Figure 3: A distinguished member of the cat family.

Figure 4: Lion's paw detail.

crushing them flat onto the floor, and yet with definite, perceptible contact. Working with that image will help your mind and therefore intensify your energetic experience of the TOUCH phase – which sets up the subsequent SURGE.

We can go further with this by incorporating *pad* imagery. In the REST phase, imagine that what's bearing your stepping leg's weight is pads like the lion's, somehow attached to your foot or shoe. They're thick and resilient in a way, and yet also soft and flexible. You should imagine that your foot's surface has that kind of padding on it, and that you support the leg's weight on such pads in your REST phase.

In the RAISE phase, be sure to mentally check the raised foot itself, for softness and total relaxation before doing any TOUCH. Then, by working with these two lion's paw images, the tufts and pads, in the TOUCH and REST phases respectively, you can greatly amplify the subsequent SURGE.

CAT-STEP: LEFT WARDOFF EXAMPLE

Figure 5: Beginning the Cat-Step transition into LEFT WARDOFF

Figure 6: Beginning the Cat-Step RAISE

Figure 7: Cat-Step RAISE

Figure 8: Cat-Step HEEL TOUCH (no weight)

Figure 9: Cat-Step HEEL REST (leg's weight only)

Figure 10: Cat-Step SOLE REST (leg's weight only), and RELAX

Figure 11: Cat-Step SURGE begins at feet

Figure 12: SURGE energy travels up legs

Figure 13: SURGE energy rises

Figure 14: SURGE energy continues to rise

Figure 15: SURGE energy extends through *ni wan* and *yin tang* areas in the head

Figure 16: SURGE energy lowers through *yuan ye* armpit points

Figure 17: SURGE energy sparks out at hands

Figure 18: LOAD begins

Figure 19: LOAD continues

Figure 20: LOAD continues

Figure 21: LOAD finishes in completed LEFT WARDOFF pose

THE COUNTER-SINK PROTOCOL

The ZMQ37 system is a set of transitions from one formally named pose to the next. The Cat-Step protocol applies to every *transition*, and the Counter-Sink protocol can be worked on every *named pose*. This implies an overall different style of practice.

We read that Tai Chi is like the infinite, unceasing flow of a great river and so on. That's a valuable basic practice mode. But too often, the emphasis on pure flow causes us to gloss over the many opportunities the form offers us to go deeply into *nei gong* (内功) internal energy work with every step or posture.

Both pure flow mode and start-stop mode are valuable. The idea of static standing for internal work is accepted in many styles of Tai Chi and other internal systems. But usually the standing methods are either too simple or too complex.

Too simple means that it becomes a purely physical endurance drill. For example, classical Shaolin 'horse stance' sitting sometimes devolves to this. Too complex means that, while standing statically, the student is required to maintain a complicated mental architecture of imaginary springs, bands, levers, pulleys, and cables, which ends by reinforcing tension.

What's needed is a specific, simple and direct method with only a moderate, minimal physical engagement (to keep the mind focused), and which furthers the unitary goal of *developing the energy*. The Counter-Sink protocol is that method, and it fits the spirit and letter of the ZMQ37 form precisely.

Go through the form sequentially at the normal moderate pace. Every time you assume a named pose, you *pause* in the given shape and very slightly *lower* yourself, to a silent count of seven. If you count at a leisurely pace, that will be anywhere from 5 to 10 seconds. The exact duration isn't important. You can adjust the count to suit yourself.

The important thing is to slightly lower yourself at a constant rate for a short duration. You don't lower in little broken stages to match the count numbering, but rather in a smooth, slow, unbroken drop as you silently count off the interval: 1.. 2.. 3.. 4.. 5.. 6.. 7. Then you continue with the transition to the next pose, as normal.

How much to lower yourself? A student who's physically stronger and more flexible can lower more than somebody older, weaker or stiffer. But the degree of actual physical drop is of little importance. A laser tape measure applied to the distance between your head and the ceiling should detect some objective lowering of your body. But it needn't be very much. This is not an athletic regimen, nor is it the '*butt scrapes floor*' low stance work found in the more theatrically oriented styles of Tai Chi. This is pure *nei gong* internal work.

Because the measurable physical lowering is so slight, we can practice "infinite lowering" with this method. Have you heard of so-called *endless* or *infinity* swimming pools? Such a pool is only a bit more than a single body length in size, but one in which you can swim any continuous distance, due to the pushback of the current.

With the Counter-Sink, there is no push-back, but you can achieve a similar feeling, as though you could continue to lower yourself without end, for an asymptotically tiny and diminishing distance. With an ordinary athletic type of squatting, your butt will eventually hit the floor. But with the Counter-Sink work, you should feel you are lowering without any break or gap, by such a small amount that you could continue the process *forever*. This feeling super-charges the energy.

The distance of lowering will typically be only a few centimeters. The important thing is the energy tempering and intensification that this simple method triggers. That can only be achieved if we treat the mental component of this as central. If you do the lowering without this mental component, you're wasting your time, as the physical training benefit will be slight and the energy won't be engaged.

You should imagine that your lowering is conditioned by the merest hint of "weight" on your body, to which you are reacting with extreme sensitivity. In the Tai Chi classics it's written as follows:

蠅蟲不能落 (yíng chóng bù néng luò)

A fly could not alight without setting you in motion

In this case, your 'motion' is straight down. Figure 22 will indelibly brand this idea onto your brain.

The mental component is also straight-forward. As you lower yourself to the count, your awareness and consciousness are applied to four areas on your body:

1. the palms and inner fingers of both hands

2. the soles of both feet

When you do that, you engage the energy flow throughout your entire body.

Figure 22: The Counter-Sink Protocol: You lower yourself slightly, at a constant rate, as though in response to a slight touch of added weight on your body.

My previous books (*Juice* and *Peng*) include a lot of details on the energy pathways and transmission points. I'm not going to repeat all that here. I'll just emphasize that if you can channel the energy all the way from the soles of your feet to the inner surface of your hands, you automatically traverse every intermediate point, including all the major hot spots identified in the previous books. It's good to have a theoretical and 'scriptural' (Tai Chi classics) awareness of certain hot spots in the human energy architecture, but for the purpose of practical *nei gong* based on ZMQ37, it's enough to work consciously with soles and palms.

I refer you again to the obscure Tai Chi classic that details the energy transmission from feet to fingers which includes the line below:

氣經掌陰面直到五指尖

The qi energy, passing across the surface of the inner hand, directly charges the five fingers

That phrase 'surface of the inner hand' (掌陰面; *zhang yin mian*, in the verse above) describes the mental target zone for the Counter -Sink. Imagine a kid smushing fingerpaints on a paper. If he raises his hands, the area smeared with paint approximates this *yin mian* term. To get started, you can use the image of the painted inner hand surface below.

The Counter-Sink protocol triggers the Counter-Sink *crystallization*. This means that as you lower yourself, with the four surfaces mentally engaged (which just means that you stay aware of them) you'll feel a structure of connected energy burst into activation throughout your entire body. Even though your mind is focused at the four terminal areas, the energy has to connect from your feet through all of you to reach your hands.

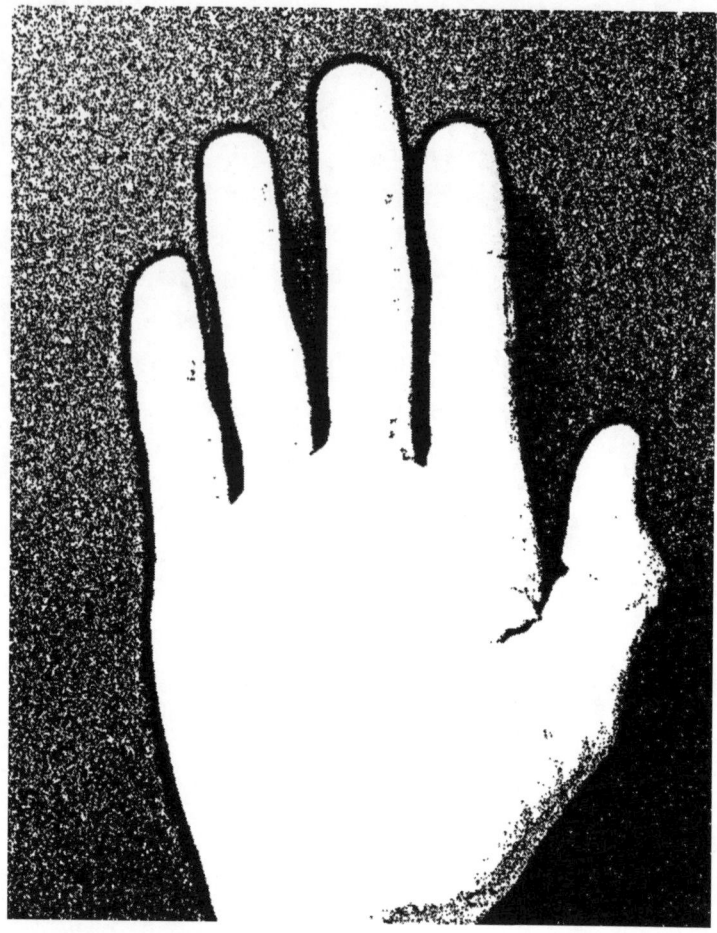

Figure 23: The *yin mian* inner hand area for energy concentration in the Counter -Sink protocol.

You'll feel this happening. The energy will seem, as Chen Weiming wrote: *'both hard and soft at the same time'*. You'll feel as though an infinity of energy 'beads' or pellets scattered throughout your body are forming up, snapping to their neighbors and regimenting them- selves into a linked lattice that has no gaps and no excesses. It feels like pure, almost inhuman power.

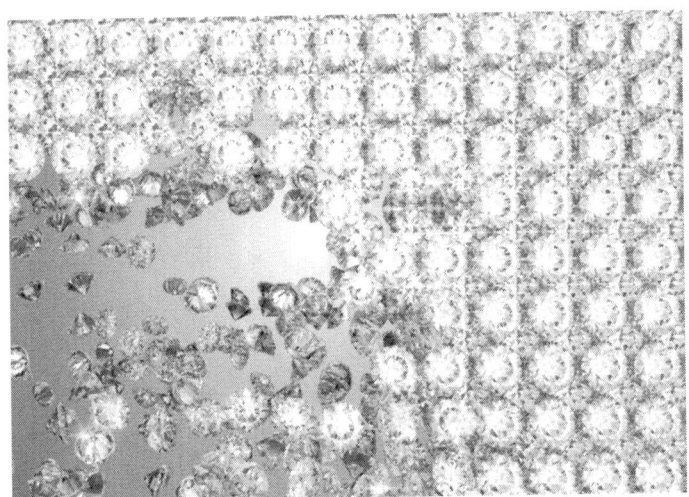

Figure 24: The Counter-Sink protocol triggers the Counter-Sink *crystallization*, a joining of scattered energy units into a single coherent lattice throughout your body.

I'm not saying you can then go out with just this and rule the Octagon as a martial artist, but don't you think it sounds interesting? Now that you have the basic idea, you can experiment on your own and see how far you can take it.

Some physical training systems include 'slow squats'. This means you slowly lower your body as far as possible, to a very slow count, then pause and slowly rise up again. The difference between that exercise and the Counter-Sink is, first of all, that in the Tai Chi sinking the degree of lowering is far less.

If you try to lower more than a few inches, you flip over into athletic mode. Athletic mode involves greater tension and physical effort, as well as mental distraction away from the energy target surfaces and into the working the drill physically. In addition, slow squats are generally done with even 50-50 weight distribution, while in the

ZMQ37 form every named pose (apart from opening and closing) always manifests the basic principle of *distinguish substantial and insubstantial*, no double weighting. But the most important difference is that the Counter-Sink enables Tai Chi players to feel the most powerful level of internal energy that many have ever felt, often after slogging through decades of pleasant but relatively barren practice.

Counter-Sink: Single Whip Example

Figure 25: COUNTER-SINK beginning in SINGLE WHIP pose, lowering from count 1

Figure 26: Lowering at count 2 – start of energy crystallization.

Figure 27: Lowering at count 3 - intensification of energy crystallization.

Figure 28: Lowering at count 4 - intensification of energy crystallization.

Figure 29: Lowering at count 5 - intensification of energy crystallization.

Figure 30: Lowering at count 6 - intensification of energy crystallization.

Figure 31: Lowering at count 7 – full intensity energy crystallization.

Figure 32: Summary of the Counter-Sink process

Duration

Working the form as this book teaches will increase your practice time, no two ways about it. If you've watched the online videos of Professor Zheng, you know that he does it fairly quickly, requiring only 5 to 7 minutes for the entire sequence. That's optimal for 'flow' or 'river' mode. The addition of the Counter-Sink on every named pose, and the Cat-Step on every transition between poses, inevitably lengthens your time.

When I'm incorporating both of these intensifier methods, the full sequence takes me about 20 minutes to complete. That's still not an exorbitant time investment on a daily basis, and, more importantly, in that 20 minutes I experience more energy amplification than hours spent working on other methods, and far beyond what can be experienced from working this same Tai Chi form in simple 'flow' or 'river' mode.

If you really need to prune it back to the original 5 to 7 minutes, I suggest that doing only the first section (up to the first Cross Hands) with Cat-Step and Counter-Sink, will be a better use of that narrow time window than flowing though the whole form but without the *nei gong* depth.

How to Work It

Take your best orgasm, multiply the feeling by twenty, and you're still fuckin miles off the pace.

- Irvine Welsh

The discussion of duration leads into the more general area of the best way to work the form overall. There are many options and you should experiment on your own. I'll review some obvious approaches here.

The most minimal way to work it is via the bare set of seven isolated poses given in the *Peng* book. One of the key methods in the *Peng* book is the *zhang zhuang* rising activation, applied to those seven basic stances. With that method, people who don't have time to practice or even learn the full ZMQ37 form can begin to build internal energy. It's a powerful method, highly compacted in time and space.

But if you have time to learn all or a good chunk of the ZMQ form, then you can take up the more articulated internal protocols of this book instead, or you can pack *all* the protocols into one unified practice set based on ZMQ37. The remainder of this book will focus on the new material in the new protocols, but the foundations are entirely as specified in the introductory sections of the *Peng* book.

If you applied all three protocols (Cat-Step, Counter-Sink, and *zhang zhuang*) to every pose and transition of the full form, you'd be getting close to 30 minutes for the full sequence. That isn't necessary though. If you have a lot of time, you can segregate your practice into the following segments:

1. 'Flow' or 'River' mode full-form, followed by

2. Full form with Cat-Step and Counter-Sink on every pose and transition, followed by

3. Isolated pose work with *zhang zhuang*

That's the most optimal program for a single training session. But any one of those segments alone could be a full and productive daily training regimen.

The main training method introduced in the Peng book is *zhang zhuang*. It's interesting – since that book has come out, it's gotten both cheers and jeers and it's certainly sold well. But no matter what else people have said about it, on the net or in private, essentially nobody has specifically commented on adopting the *zhang zhuang*, and trying to make it work. So I gather that neither friend nor foe is actually drilling that for real. Which is a pity because it's a training of unearthly power. I guess it's too brilliantly radical for this dark age, the Kali Yuga...

But really, you only have to get the knack. The key to the *zhang zhuang* practice is that as you do the *microreactivation* (straightening) thing, while the physical foundation is your one strong (*yang* or substantial) leg from which you begin the straightening, you keep full mental awareness of *both legs at once*. Feel the huge contrast between the strength of the *yang* leg vs. the weakness and emptiness of the *yin* leg. Then **wow** you'll see how this drill turns your whole body into a plutonium bomb of internal radiation, especially when combined with the stuff in this book. The most advanced

ZMQ37 practice of them all is a variant of *zhang zhuang* discussed in the chapter *Advanced Work*, below.

If your time is limited, you may want to practice only the first section of the ZMQ form (ending with the first Crossed Hands pose) incorporating only Cat-Step and Counter-Sink. That takes about 1/3 the time of the full form.

BARRIERS, HANG-UPS, IMPEDIMENTS

The biggest impediment to getting into this practice is, ironically, *general prior knowledge.* In other words, the attitude that *I'm already doing this, I already know this.* Obviously the notions of the Cat-Step and sitting low in poses are the very essence and foundation of Tai Chi, and amply discussed in the Tai Chi classic writings. So does that mean you're justified in taking a *been-there-done-that* attitude to the Cat-Step and Counter-Sink protocols?

No. You are emphatically *not* justified in taking that attitude. I don't say that as a marketing thing or brand differentiation to sell my own stuff. It's a technical and empirical point, worth examining in some detail. I'll consider this *foreknowledge* hang-up here, as the most practical of the impediments. Additional barriers of a more conceptual nature are treated in the chapter *Refund Policy*, below.

To enliven the discussion, let's consider a straw man figure, an enthusiastic Tai Chi student, say somebody who's been learning for about two years. This would be an advanced beginner, some-body who's learned the form well from a skilled teacher with a respectable lineage. We'll call our student Ichabod Johnson, or IJ for short.

IJ does the form daily, rigorously, and thinks he knows all about Cat -Step and sitting low. Aren't those things obvious? Aren't they in the Classics? And IJ has a good natural strength in his legs, so he can sit plenty low enough already, thank you very much. No need for this 'Counter-Sink' BS!

As for Cat-Step, that's even more obvious to IJ – his teacher has many times emphasized to him the crucial importance of never putting weight into his step while transitioning to the next pose, and of testing periodically after stepping – raising his foot slightly to guarantee to himself that he's done it right.

There are two problems here, one technical and one empirical. Technically, the above *general* approach to the Cat-Step, while not wrong, is not the same thing as the CSP described here. The CSP is absolutely precise, and each stage must be felt distinctly on both the physical and energetic levels. Raise, Touch, Rest, Relax, Load. *Each phase must be engaged consciously and clearly.*

Most Tai Chi students aren't doing the Cat-Step at all. IJ, by hypothesis, is a little better, because he's trying to step without weight before loading, and even testing once in a while. But he isn't precisely distinguishing each phase. That's the technical problem in the Cat-Step area.

The technical problem in the Counter-Sink area comes from IJ's same assumption: *I already do or know this.* With naturally strong legs, IJ feels that he's already sitting very low. Lower than any of his classmates. His butt practically scrapes the floor already! What's more, IJ *maintains* that same low level throughout his execution of the form, as though practicing in a very low-ceilinged room. What more could anybody want?

But that isn't the point of the Counter-Sink. It's not about the absolute degree of physical depth at all. What gives the Counter-Sink its power is that it's a *process*, not a *state*. Staying low all through yields *less* internal energy than the very subtle lowering process (with energetic targets) specified by the Counter-Sink. So, you get no Counter-Sink points for scraping your butt on the floor.

And the technical problems lead to this empirical problem: Despite his fore-knowledge and daily application, *IJ isn't yet feeling the Cat-Step SURGE or the Counter-Sink crystallization.* These two phenomena (two versions of the soft wave of *peng* energy) are clear and distinct experiences that should be occurring strongly and unequivocally on every single change of either foot's PAW (Position, Angle, Weighting for the Cat-Step), and also when assuming every named pose (for the Counter-Sink).

Since IJ has never experienced the SURGE or Crystallization, and all the less in connection with any kind of stepping or lowering protocol, he doesn't really feel any lack. He's happy with the Tai Chi experience that he has. And he's confident that with another 30 or 40 years of dedicated practice, he'll begin to experience the internal energy laid out in the Tai Chi classic writings. But 30 or so years later, when finally he's begun to feel the faintest stirring of what I'm talking about here, he may then remember that somebody (me) laid it all out openly, a long time before. It could have been straightforwardly accessed within a few months of moderate training. Bottom line, anybody who isn't feeling the *empirical results* of the Cat-Step and Counter-Sink still hasn't truly incorporated or understood the methods.

These protocols aren't "shortcuts" (that's a disparaging attack word). They're just good, efficient practice methods for internal energy. Of course, like any training method, they require intelligent and sustained application over time.

POSE NOTES

I've said you can't learn the poses from this book or any other. So there's no point in my publishing a long photo section here. Nobody would ever look at it, and if they *looked* at it, that's *all* they'd do. They wouldn't work through it diligently.

That's human nature. How many martial arts photo books do you own? And of those, how many have you drilled through in learning mode, aping every move and grokking it all by working through the text and looking at the pics? And integrated that learning into your daily practice? Right. Thought so. Same goes for DVD's. Pics will make the book twice as long and nobody will follow them anyway.

But for this chapter, I do want to list out all the poses, in order. The great value here is for those who already know, or are presently learning, the ZMQ37 sequence. If those people even casually browse this section, they'll find many 24K nuggets of rare and valuable training advice, covering aspects of posture, movement, and mechanics, but oriented, as always, mostly toward the energetics. Practitioners of other styles will also benefit by seeing how the abstract methods are applied in various situations.

Don't bypass this chapter lightly. I can almost guarantee that any serious student of ZMQ37 will find at least one practice idea that's a real eye-opener (but if you *don't* find anything good, please read the chapter *Refund Policy* before self-immolating in your anger, hurt, and disappointment).

If you're going to integrate the two deep practice principles of this book (Cat-Step and Counter-Sink) you'll need this section's guidance for how to get the most from the specifics of the program. But reading these Notes straight through may be heavy going. You may want to browse them casually, or spot check a given pose or transition that you're wondering about.

One great feature of ZMQ37 is its precise and logical geometric layout. Every named pose has a direction label: North, South, East, West, Northeast, Northwest, Southeast, or Southwest. You will always be precisely aligned on one of those eight vectors. If you don't know what direction you're supposed to be aligned with, at every point of the form, you haven't deeply learned the real ZMQ37. I'm going to assume a South-facing start position.

By "aligned" I mean *the direction toward which your nose and waist both face.* That's another great logical feature of the ZMQ37: your waist is always precisely in-line with, and square-on to, the overall postural vector. Your waist never diverges from the posture direction, unlike other types of Tai Chi where the waist is canted all over the place. ZMQ37 is structured with consistent logical precision. Even without specific correction, you can usually work out the details of shape and transition for many poses just by thinking logically and analytically, using basic knowledge of the principles.

The form divides naturally into two sections. Section 1 is one-third of the total moves. These moves are somewhat easier to perform physically than the moves in Section 2. Many Section 1 poses occur multiple times throughout the form as a whole.

For Section 1, my notes in this chapter are more comprehensive, in terms of movement mechanics. Stuff like: *'right arm here, left foot there'.* In addition to that external stuff, I emphasize the integration of Cat-Step and Counter-Sink.

For Section 2, I back off from the minute descriptions of external details of postures and transitions. You will have gotten the basic idea from the Section 1 explanations. To go much deeper into the mechanics, you'll need to either learn from a live-action teacher or follow Professor Zheng's YouTube performances at half-speed playback, with his book close at hand (see Bibliography). In Section 2, under each posture's heading, I point out particularly interesting or useful features in the application of the internal protocols to the context of that specific move.

This book is a *sui generis* attempt to coach the internal conditioning of the ZMQ system without having to take on the heavy lifting of teaching the actual poses. Whether or not I can succeed at making that useful, who knows? But if I hit every pitch I'm not swinging hard enough. What the hell. I'll give it a shot.

Section 1

0 無極勢 (wú jí shì)
Unlimited
(South)

1 預備勢 (yù bèi shì)
Preparation
(South)

In the simple transition from Pose 0 to Pose 1, we can experience the following:

- SOLE version of Cat-Step,
- Cat-Step SURGE,
- Counter-Sink *crystallization*

This simple transition has it all. It's exactly as Robert W. Smith, my first Tai Chi teacher, used to say: *"In any spiritual discipline, everything is contained in the first lesson"*.

Begin with feet together; toes 30 degrees outward. Stand upright and relaxed, hands hanging normally at your sides. Sink all your weight into the right leg until your left leg feels empty, then step left foot out to the left side at shoulder-width, straight and level. Since this is our first Cat-Step, it's worth going over in minute detail.

RAISE: Keep your foot suspended in the air, toes pointed straight forward, just centimeters from the floor. Try to relax your leg as much as possible while holding the foot up. Relax your ankle even while keeping the foot straight and level.

Turn your raised foot slightly inward, so that the toes point straight ahead, to 'correct' for the original outward splay of 30 degrees.

TOUCH: Place the sole of your left foot barely in contact with the floor, no weight. Feel how much or how little leg tension is required to maintain this.

REST: As you release all tension from the left leg, allow the floor to support the weight of the leg alone. All other body weight is still completely supported by your right leg. If you bend your right leg a bit more, you'll feel the weight of the left leg more clearly.

RELAX: With mind and awareness, check your left leg briefly to feel whether there is any tension left in it at all. Your right leg should be supporting all your weight, except that the weight of the *left leg itself* rests completely on the floor. Check toes, ankle, calf, knee area, thigh, and butt for absolute relaxation of the entire leg.

SURGE: Somewhere between the REST and RELAX phase, the Cat-Step SURGE will suddenly blow through your body, from both feet up to and through your torso, across and over your head, and down into your arms. It may take a few weeks of practice to feel this. At first it will be a subtle sensation, but you *will* eventually feel the pay-off. Getting to the SURGE experience, and then strengthening its energy via the Counter-Sink, are the main points of this book.

After the SURGE has washed through you, gently shift your weight to the middle, so it's 50-50 equal between left and right. Form Beautiful Lady's Hands (as described in the *Peng* book, a straight flat wrist with softly extended fingers) in three stages:

1. Move arms forward a few degrees

2. Rotate arms, so that backs of hands face forward

3. Extend fingers gently

Now, having formed the *Yubeishi* shoulder-width 50-50 startup pose, we'll attempt our first Counter-Sink.

Lower yourself gently straight down, to a silent count of 7. The count will give you roughly 5 to 10 seconds of gradual, easy sinking. Nothing dramatic, little more than a *feeling* or *impression* of sinking, but you should end up measurably lower than when you began. This is the Counter-Sink Protocol. As you lower, keep your mental awareness at (i) the *soles* of your feet and (ii) the *inner surfaces* of your palms and fingers(掌陰面)

This simple procedure for getting into *Yubeishi* incorporates the two main training features of this entire program.

2 起勢 (qǐ shì)
Commencement
(South)

This is an arm-raising method for smoothing the energy through your whole body, a kind of energetic warmup thing. Long term practice of this conditions your arms' internal energy so that they become extremely difficult for opponents to grab, lock, or to use against you in submissions.

I'm not going to show a photo sequence because nobody would follow it. The Professor has demonstrated this in videos all over Youtube. The basic mechanics are as below:

1. Raise arms to shoulder height

2. Drop elbows to retract arms

3. Relax wrist completely

4. Sink hands

5. Drop fingers

There are five wrist changes. This means that the angle formed by the hand and the lower forearm (in the wrist area) will become more open or closed five times. For ease of writing, I'll call that angle the WARP (if you must have a spell-out for every acronym: Wrist Angle of Raising Procedure). The WARP angle begins flat, 180 degrees, because that's the default straightness of the Beautiful Lady's Hand shape.

Imagine you're standing in water up to your neck. That will give you the idea of gentle resistance to your raising and lowering. If there were strings attached to your wrists from above, for move (1) they'd pull your arms up to shoulder height, shoulder width. As they reeled your arms up, since the strings are attached at the wrists, your WARP would change as the water pressure resists against the backs of your hands. This creates a slight bend in your wrist, WARP change (1).

Then, you let your elbows sink into the surrounding water. In that process, the water beneath your palms will slightly support your hands, and keep them from lowering at the same rate as your elbows. That produces WARP change (2), a slight opening of the angle created by the previous move.

Once your elbows are completely folded, your wrists will be right in front of your shoulders. At this point the slightly opened WARP angle from the prior move will naturally close, if you simply allow your wrists to relax maximally. It's a very pleasant feeling of total release. This is WARP change (3).

Now it's time to lower. This is the phase where, for the first time in my life, I actually felt the internal energy of Tai Chi, and freaked myself out. Imagine that as you lower your arms, if your wrists are relaxed enough, the water will waft up or lift your lowering fingers. It's an interesting effect where your *arms* are lowering while your *fingers* rise – but they don't rise by conscious effort. They rise because the imaginary water is gently resisting your arms' downward pressure. This is WARP change (4), a large opening of the WARP angle.

At the bottom, when the lowering is complete, your arms have returned to the original *Yubeishi* position near your sides (though very slightly fronted). The water no longer provides any resistance as your arm lowering movement ceases. Because the water doesn't resist, and because your wrists are totally relaxed (aren't they? Check them!), your fingers must slowly drop through the water. They end pointing slightly forward of straight down, which was the beginning Beautiful Lady's Hand position. This slight flattening of the hand at the end is WARP change (5).

3 攔雀尾：左掤 (lán què wěi：zuǒ péng)
Grasp sparrow tail: ward-off (left)
(South)

This is our first 70/30 pose. 70/30 means 70% of your weight on the front leg (left leg in this case) and 30% on the right. In the *Peng* book I suggested that a mental image of 80/20 is even better, because your mental target always exceeds what you can really do, physically. So a mental target of 70/30 for most people cashes out to 60/40 or even 50/50. 80/20 helps you resist that natural tendency.

It's also better for your energy. The more clearly you can *distinguish substantial vs. insubstantial*, as the Tai Chi classis constantly stress, the more internal power you can develop. With 80/20, you will feel that your front leg is doing significantly more work than the right. If your front thigh isn't burning way more than your rear thigh in "70/30" front-weighted poses, you're not separating weight cleanly enough.

The final reason for thinking in terms of 80/20 is that it conceptually unifies the front-weighted and back-weighted poses. With 70/30 for front stances vs. 100/0 for back-weighted, we end up with a gross asymmetry. That's how it's usually taught. But if we make two sensible adjustments, we can prettify this picture. The first adjustment was covered above, think of front-weighted poses as 80/20. The "20%" in that formula is the back leg's own weight, alone. In *Peng* I cited research showing that a single leg is about 20% of a human body's overall weight. That's where the 20% comes from – in these front-weighted poses, *the rear leg is mainly doing balance assistance*, not actually bearing significant body weight.

This 80/20 idea may be too radical for some people. I understand... and I have a thoughtfully considered answer: *Bye! Don't let the door smack your butt on the way out!* If I can't get radical now, in the service of helping a few serious/curious souls to feel the real stuff, then when can I?

As for the 2nd adjustment necessary to logically unify and prettify the picture, we'll get to that when we hit our first real (not transitional) back-weighted posture, a bit further on in the form.

As you get into Left Peng (the current pose) you have a chance to practice *two* Cat-Steps. Keep to the policy of never passing up any chance to practice a Cat-Step and feel the SURGE, anywhere in the form. That's the way to maximize your precious practice time.

After shifting weight all the way to left leg, when you turn your right foot outward by pivoting on the heel, you could directly LOAD weight and go on from there. But that would be neglecting a Cat -Step opportunity. What you'll do instead is RAISE your right foot into the air a few centimeters, right there "in place" where you pivoted on the heel. Then place either the entire sole (TOUCH SOLE) or just the heel (TOUCH HEEL) on the floor – no weight. This is your TOUCH phase. If you do the HEEL TOUCH, continue with HEEL REST and SOLE REST, then RELAX. When those prior stages have been clearly performed and mentally checked you'll feel the SURGE. Then and only then should you proceed with a LOAD onto the right leg.

Now you step directly straight forward with the left foot. This necessarily entails a RAISE so we're all set for another natural Cat-Step. This will definitely be a HEEL TOUCH, then REST, RELAX, feel the SURGE, and LOAD as you re-position your arms.

Normally, from here, you'd keep on with the form, if you were in river/flow mode. If you were in *zhan zhuang* mode, you'd sit statically. But in this book we do things differently. So, having assumed Left Peng, you're ready for the first true Counter-Sink interval.

Making sure of your 80/20 front/rear weight distribution, mentally count to seven as you feel yourself very slightly sinking straight down, deeper into the pose. Remember the general principles that guide all Counter-Sink work: the mental energy targets are your "fingerpaint hand" surfaces and the soles of both feet.

4 攔雀尾：右挪 (lán què wěi：yòu péng)
Grasp sparrow tail: ward-off (right)
(West)

This is another transition that calls for a full HEEL version of the Cat -Step, so do that with your right foot. This is not a stationary Cat-Step because you will need to RAISE your right foot anyway, to shift it a bit sideways, to the right. After positioning your foot above the floor at the place where you want to plant it, continue with a normal HEEL Cat-Step. Feel the SURGE, and then LOAD the right leg with 80% of your body weight. Do the Counter-Sink.

5 攔雀尾：捋 (lán què wěi： lǚ)
Grasp sparrow's tail: roll back
(West)

Rotate waist first to your right for the Rollback gesture, then back leftward. As you extend your left arm toward the Southeast corner, you can begin your Cat-Step. Note that once again, a Cat-Step is not strictly required at this point - it's not a Position change, merely a Weighting change. But I've said elsewhere that *any* change of your PAW (Position, Angle, Weighting) calls for another full Cat-Step protocol. Maximize your practice time!

You can do this as either a HEEL or SOLE Cat-Step, up to you. This is a stationary Cat-Step, triggered by change of weighting alone. So your foot stays at/above exactly the same place throughout.

6 攔雀尾：擠 (lán què wěi： jǐ)
Grasp sparrow's tail: press
(West)

This is the LOAD condition following the Rollback above. Do the Counter-Sink to a count of 7. As your hands touch where they cross at the inner wrists, you can still do the mental awareness part of the Counter-Sink as usual – mind on the inside surfaces of the palms and fingers ("fingerpaint" hands).

7 攔雀尾：按 (lán què wěi： àn)
Grasp sparrow's tail: push
(West)

To begin this you sit straight back on your left leg from the Press move just completed. Your fingers/hands remain in place, just as though they were clipped *in situ*. Therefore, your arms must naturally lengthen as you sit back. Sitting back involves a weighting change that tells us: time to inject another Cat-Step. We take every chance to do that. Since this is a stationary Cat-Step, after the RAISE you can replace your foot with either the direct SOLE version or the HEEL then SOLE version. Feel the SURGE, then LOAD as you push forward gently. Most of the push action is coming from your body going forward, and very little from actual arm extension. After finishing the outward-going push, lower gently into the Counter-Sink.

8 單鞭 (dān biān)
Single whip
(East)

Now you come to a large, sweeping kind of step. Basically you need to step halfway around a circle so that you end up facing East from the previous West-facing pose. Because this step is too big to handle in one go, it's broken into smaller foot and weighting shifts.

You sit straight back, with that feeling again of fingers 'clipped' in place, so that your arms gently straighten. Then rotate to the right (always begin rotations with waist movement, not arms). You rotate your right foot in place, on the heel. This is now an interesting potential Cat-Step situation. The right foot has become weightless. That's a Weighting change, and according to the PAW principle, should call for a Cat-Step practice.

You may feel cramped, because your right foot is torqued so severely leftward that it almost bumps up against your left foot. The narrowness of this transitional shape makes it hard to go through the whole Cat-Step protocol with the usual precision. If it's too hard to do every stage clearly, take as much body weight off the right leg as possible, and try to relax the whole leg. Eventually after some weeks or months of practice, even this awkward, partial Cat-Step will trigger a great SURGE experience.

You then sit all weight back to the right as you bend your elbows and form the hook with your right hand, held at chest level directly over your left palm facing upward beneath.

With all weight on the right, you are now ready to take a wide step leftward with your left foot. This is the first of what I call "wide angle" steps. That means it's a Cat-Step situation whose mechanics call for a step greater than shoulder width. This is a fantastic opportunity to practice your relaxation and overall loosening.

Be sure to extend your right hook hand adequately far outward to the right side, for balance. Then step your left foot widely to the left side so that you can end up in a sufficiently wide, shoulder-width front stance (80/20) at the end, without having to shuffle your feet (cheating!) The RAISE is the natural step required by the sequence, but you may find the TOUCH phase difficult. To keep only the barest floor contact without any weight on the left foot may be tough at first.

The key is to begin the step with your upper body, especially shoulders, totally relaxed. This move is a good chance for self-testing what Aiki Daito Grandmaster Sagawa Yukiyoshi always stressed: *No power or tension in shoulders.* Here you can check that without needing a push-hands partner to diagnose you from the outside. If you wobble, or can't do a weightless TOUCH with a full step and a good final foot position, you need to work on relaxation.

Relax the stepping leg and foot as much as possible, do a light HEEL TOUCH with no weight, then apply the leg weight to the HEEL, then gently lay down the full SOLE, maintaining the leg weight only (no body weight yet). Finally, as your left hand, waist, and rear (right) foot all rotate eastward into final position, you LOAD 80% body weight forward into the left leg.

Now you can do your Counter-Sink. The Counter-Sink experience of energy crystallization (as explained earlier) is more profound in this pose than in any other. That may be why this pose is duplicated so often in the sequence. You will also feel a strong (but very pleasant) internal energy pressure arising from your lower body and enveloping your entire upper body, torso and arms.

The left hand is engaged at the palm/fingers surface (*yin mian*). When doing the Counter-Sink in this pose, you may wonder how to mentally engage the right hand, because this is our first example of a non-standard hand shape. You should mentally engage the right *as a whole*. That is, you are mentally aware of the entire hook-hand shape as a relaxed blob of energy (like the song Comfortably Numb: "*...my hands felt just like two balloons*"). We will also use this general idea again when later poses call for the 'Beautiful Lady's Fist' hand shape.

Single Whip can also serve as a diagnostic for advanced relaxation. When you form the hook hand, your fingertips (including your thumb), must all touch one another, uniformly. No cheating! And they must be almost straight. Now, if you're forming the correct shape, use your left hand to touch the large bulge of meat on the inner/rear of the hook hand, at the base of your thumb. If you are like most people, that bulge of meat is pretty tense and hard right now.

The amazing thing is – my teacher's hook-hand, all over including that bulge - is totally relaxed. It's like *tofu*. I've never stopped being amazed at that. I've tested hundreds of people on this and never found anybody else who could remain relaxed in the correct shape (plenty of sneaks though, who try to cheat around it). He's the only one to accomplish it – so far. But the next one could be *you*. So keep working on relaxation, eyes on the prize.

9 提手 (tí shǒu)
Raise arms
(South)

You will now assume your first true back-weighted pose. Traditionally, it is said that the back-weighted poses have a 100/0 rear/front weight distribution. Well, yes and no. We are going to apply the Cat-Step and Counter-Sink, as always, so we're going to creatively tweak that simple ratio a little bit, in the interest of squeezing every particle of internal power and experience from your limited practice time. There's no time in this human lifespan for doing anything woodenly, to a mindless formula.

But we keep well within the spirit of the traditional idea of back weighting and *distinguishing substantial vs. insubstantial.*

The mechanics are simple. From your 80/20 Single Whip, put all your weight into your left leg, while opening your arms to 90 degrees or a bit more. You re-form your right hand back to Beautiful Lady's Hand. Now that you've got 100% of your weight on the left, you've fulfilled the letter of the law, which requires a total separation of weight for this transition.

Pivot your right foot on the front/toe area of your shoe. Then, move your foot leftward to narrower than shoulder-width, such that your right heel touches the floor at a spot where it would barely graze your left heel if you drew it straight back. This is done as you gently hug your arms inward to the Raise Arms position, left palm facing right elbow, waist facing front (South).

You'll have to get the detailed external mechanics from your teacher or, best of all, from watching the ZMQ YouTube videos. I'm covering the energetics only here.

This pose calls for a PARTIAL Cat-Step. That means it creates a pose that doesn't end with a standard LOAD. That's a back-weighted pose. But it's close to a normal Cat-Step, in that you do RAISE your foot to bring it inward/leftward, you do a HEEL TOUCH, and then... what?

There's a choice here. You have now achieved the pose, so you could do your Counter-Sink with either the TOUCH condition (no weight at all in the right leg, neither body weight nor leg weight). If you do that, you are fulfilling the "letter of the law" in that it's a pure 100/0 split. That's fine for your Counter-Sink process.

However, if you do that, you've pretty much missed a chance to experience a SURGE. And we don't want to miss any chance for that. So an alternative is to do the HEEL TOUCH as above, but then follow it with the HEEL REST condition. This allows you to relax the leg muscles, even that small bit of tension that had been used to keep any weight off the leg in the prior TOUCH. When you relax the leg for the heel REST, you'll feel the SURGE, just as in a normal Cat-Step.

You can then do your Counter-Sink from this configuration, same as you could from the TOUCH situation above.

10靠 (kào)
lean
(South)

This is a black sheep pose, a rare exception to the general ZMQ property that waist, nose and lead foot all point in the pose's main direction (South in this case). Here, the foot points South and the general line of the pose is southward, but due to the shape of the shoulder strike, the waist is oriented eastward. That's because you have to turn a bit sideways to apply your shoulder. In the final strike, your left fingers (in Beautiful Lady's Hand) point directly to the back of your right elbow, with your right arm extended straight down. Try to feel as though your left hand is energetically "supporting" (without actually touching) your right arm.

This pose can be confusing, because to mount a truly effective shoulder strike you'd probably have to lean a bit. At the least, to really hit a target, your front knee would probably have to go a bit past the toe of your front foot. But in this pose, you don't want to do that. In this pose, more than in any other, your front knee must be held precisely and directly above your front toe.

Do not let your front knee cave inward or bow outward. Caving inward (to the left) is the most common fault here and it can be injurious to your knee over a long habitual time. So try to resist the temptation to lean forward, or toward any other direction. Stick with the basic principle *Body Upright*. We aren't cage fighting with this, at least not today.

As you get into this pose, you have an opportunity to practice another partial Cat-Step before the full Cat-Step that forms the final pose. So you withdraw your right foot, all the way back, past the supporting left. That is a natural RAISE condition, then you do the TOUCH with the toe or front part of your shoe. No weight.

Now you have another optional situation. You can go directly from the back TOUCH to the final full frontward Cat-Step (which leads to the full and final shoulder strike). Or, you could REST the right foot while it's in back there, and experience another Cat-Step SURGE. Your call.

Either way, you will at some point step forward again with your right foot, leaving only a half shoulder-width distance for the final stance (another exceptional property of this pose – it's only half the width of a standard 70/30). Do a full regular HEEL Cat-Step, and end by feeling the SURGE and doing the LOAD. Then do your 7-count Counter-Sink.

11 白鶴亮翅 (bái hè liàng chì)
White crane spreads wings
(East)

This is the pose on the front cover of this book. From the shouldering, you rotate your waist eastward while raising your right hand into an Army type salute. The right hand is canted at 45 degrees, not flat down and not rotated too far upward. The left arm is gently extended downward, but as always in this type of gentle downward extension, don't let your arm energetically "die".

There's a tendency to focus so much on the hand where the action seems to be (in this case the right), that the "off" hand is allowed to energetically wither. Doing the Counter-Sink protocol in this pose will entirely eliminate that problem, because in the Counter-Sink, *both* hands are *always* mentally engaged (*yin mian* "fingerpaint" hand surfaces).

12 摟膝拗步 (lōu xī ào bù)
Brush knee twist step
(East)

Getting into this pose requires a Cat-Step, and the SURGE from this one is really good, one of the best. So do it slowly, precisely, and carefully as always. You step out with your left foot, do the:

- HEEL TOUCH

- HEEL REST

- SOLE REST

- RELAX

... then feel the SURGE before the LOAD.

When getting into this pose, be sure to actually "brush *knee*". I emphasize that because there's a tendency to just wave the left hand *over* the knee, rather than truly passing the inner left palm *across* the face of the bent left knee. When people let the hand brush too high like that, my teacher always admonishes them: *This pose isn't Brush Thigh!*

In some extreme cases, we have to admonish: *This isn't Brush Waist!* The reason this problem happens is that a lot of people don't respect the conditions for the front-weighted stance in ZMQ37 (traditionally called 70/30, or 80/20 in this book). That configuration requires you to keep your inguinal crease well bent, the thigh as close to parallel to the floor as you can, sitting low with the front knee directly above your front toe. If you do all that, you will naturally brush the knee, without making any special effort.

But if your stance does not yet allow you to naturally accomplish this, it's better to Brush Thigh (or Brush Waist) rather than lean forward with your upper body to get it. The general principles, like Body Upright, generally trump the pose-specific requirements. Once you've settled into the pose, do your Counter-Sink as always.

13 手揮琵琶 (shǒu huī pípá)
Hand strums the pipa
(East)

A *pipa* is a Chinese lute. We've come to a special juncture in the sequence. Between the previous pose (Brush Knee) and this one, there's an unnamed crypto-move. But any move that requires a change of PAW in your feet is a chance to do yet another Cat-Step.

This won't be just any Cat-Step. This crypto-move will give you the chance to do your first full REAR Cat-Step. It's pretty simple mechanically, but you may find that the REAR Cat-Step will trigger an even stronger final SURGE than the front Cat-Steps do.

All you need to do is shift your weight completely forward, into the already dominant/substantial left leg. There will be a natural tendency to lean your upper body forward into the move, but resist that. *Body Upright*, even here. You can optionally do a 1-legged Counter-Sink into your left leg here, with your right foot suspended behind.

As you transfer all weight into the left, your right foot will become completely un-weighted and will almost seem to float up off the floor on its own. Allow that to happen, as that is a natural RAISE condition. Then, re-touch your toe, or the front part of your shoe, at exactly the spot where it just lifted up. This is only a TOUCH – no weight at all, at first. Then, keeping the same toe-contact position of your foot, allow the leg's own weight, and only that weight, to come into the toe and be supported by the floor. Check to make sure you've really done both the preceding TOUCH, and this front REST stage, fully and precisely.

Then, though this may be a little challenging at first, you need to kind of roll your foot backward so that you get the entire SOLE in REST mode on the floor. This is tricky because you may find yourself beginning to prematurely transfer body weight rearward, into the right leg. But you have to stay with the leg's own weight *only* at this point. The deeper you bend the supporting left leg, the easier it will be to maintain the leg's weight only in this full-sole REST condition.

From the sole REST, relax your leg completely. With the back step, you can feel and control the relaxation of leg muscles you may have overlooked in the preceding frontward Cat-Steps. In particular, the back of your thigh and your butt must be mentally checked for relaxation. As you do this RELAX phase, you will experience probably the most intense whole-body Cat-Step SURGE so far.

You then transfer all weight to the right foot (LOAD) and re-assume the same pose as the Raise Hands that followed Single Whip, but it's now on the other side and has a different name. Again you have a choice either to remain truly 100/0 with a TOUCH condition, or do the TOUCH with your right foot but then go one more step into the heel REST, then RELAX the leg as much as possible and feel the SURGE. Finally, do your 1-legged Counter-Sink here too.

14 搂膝拗步 (lōu xī ào bù)
Brush knee twist step
(East)

This is a repeat of exactly the previous occurrence of Brush Knee, and all the same comments apply.

15 進步搬攔捶 (jìn bù bān lán chuí)
Advance, deflect, parry and punch
(East)

Getting into this pose from the previous one is tricky, and proceeds in a few distinct steps.

First, you retract all weight to your right (rear) foot, as you rotate your waist to the left and bring your hands to your left side near your waist. The left arm is extended gently downward, with the hand remaining in Beautiful Lady's Hand shape. But the right hand now becomes what I call 'Beautiful Lady's Fist'. It has the same flat, straight wrist, but the fingers are curled into a very gentle, soft fist shape. It should appear as a well-shaped, practical hitting fist from the outside. It isn't sloppily open or obviously loose. But if somebody were to touch it, it would feel totally soft. The inner wrists of both left and right hands face one another at your left side.

Then, you step leftward with your foot opening outward at 45 degrees. This is a Cat-Step, but it's only a slight foot repositioning for the purpose of opening the foot in preparation for the next big move. Use the SOLE step. RAISE the foot, place the SOLE down in a TOUCH, then REST, RELAX, and feel the SURGE. Then LOAD 100% onto your left foot. Through this step your arms remain down by your left hip, left palm facing right fist, with about the width of a basketball between them.

From there, you will take *another* Cat-Step, this time with the right foot, slightly out to the right side, one shoulder-width distance forward. This is a substantial move so you apply the HEEL version of the Cat-Step. That means you RAISE as usual, position your foot above the spot where you'll drop it, then TOUCH with heel only, no weight, barely *touching* the fur tufts on your paw....

Then allow the leg's weight (only) to flow into the support of the floor, that is your REST, still on your heel. Then continue the REST condition by softly dropping the front part of the sole onto the floor. Then further RELAX your whole leg to the max, toes to butt. You will feel that huge internal power SURGE from your feet blasting right out through your arms. Throughout this rightward/forward step your arms remain as they were in the previous stage.

Now the final step in setting up this pose. Your right foot is going to be the rear foot in the final pose. So you need to LOAD it with 100% body weight as you step forward yet again, this time with your left foot into the final stance.

As you step forward with your de-weighted left foot, your right arm (fist) makes a small circle in front of your chest, and as you place down your foot and begin to load body weight into it, your left arm (open hand) makes a bigger outside circle in a diagonal downward chopping motion across the high front of an imaginary opponent. It resembles *kesa giri* in Japanese swordsmanship.

After completing the left hand 'chop', as you begin to LOAD weight onto the left foot, you punch out from below your waist with the right fist, straight along your front centerline. Your left hand withdraws slightly such that your left palm ends up facing your right elbow. This is the final shape, so now you can do your Counter-Sink.

This is your first Counter-Sink with a fist shape (right hand). Just as we did for Single Whip, you don't have the open 'inner palm and fingers' surface to work with. As you sink, place your mind as always in the soles of your feet, and the inner surface of the left hand. For the right hand, place your mental awareness on the overall fist as such. It's like the song lyric quoted earlier for Single Whip: '*my hands felt just like two balloons*'.

16 如封似閉 (rú fēng sì bì)
Apparent closing
(East)

This pose is badly named, it could be better called 'Withdraw and Push'. It's a fairly complex little mini-sequence, consisting of a setup technique followed by a double-handed push.

The basic mechanics involve a *left-right-left* series of three waist turns to power the technique. Remember that in all techniques of the ZMQ form, the initial physical impetus always begins with your waist, not your arms. This Withdraw and Push technique is peerless for helping you get your head firmly around that concept.

Turn your waist leftward to the left corner as you slip your right hand beneath your upper right arm, triceps area, left palm facing inward. Your right arm will be carried leftward by the waist movement alone, but it should also extend somewhat, to accommodate the left hand slipping under.

Then, turn your waist back rightward as you draw the left hand forward along the outside line of the withdrawing right arm. The rightward waist turn has created the movement of withdrawal. It's as though you are wiping off an opponent's grip on your right elbow area. This may not seem practical, but let's just say that when demonstrated as an application by my teacher, everybody in the audience goes away ... convinced. You end that move with both palms at shoulder height by your right side, palms facing inward.

Then turn your waist back straight frontwards, as you bring your hands to chest level and rotate both palms to face forward in preparation for another standard push, which we've already seen as Pose 7 above but with the feet reversed as we're now left-foot forward.

You can sneak one Cat-Step into the above sequence. It's one of those freebies, not strictly required by the foot positioning of the pose sequence. But we have our policy of using any opportunity to train the Cat-Step and feel the SURGE, because with every SURGE you experience, your internal conditioning is becoming stronger.

So we slip in a stationary Cat-Step here, after the left hand has gone under the right upper arm, and you've completed the 'wipe' with the rightward waist turn. The waist turn back to center is about to begin, with your hands at shoulder height to your right side, both palms facing inward.

At that point you can pause and do your stationary Cat-Step. Your weight is 100% back on your right foot, so it's easy to RAISE your left foot. Then, TOUCH back down with the SOLE version of Cat-Step in the same place you raised from (that's why this type is called stationary Cat-Step). From TOUCH, transition to REST (whole sole), then RELAX, and feel your SURGE. Only then do you LOAD and continue with your frontward push, into your 80/20 front stance (Pose 7, *an*).

17 十字手 (shí zì shǒu)
Cross hands
(South)

We've come to the end of the First Section, with Cross Hands. You'll turn your waist and left foot southwards to face your original starting direction, as you open your arms and then circle them together.

Begin by shifting all weight back to your right foot as you turn your waist rightwards, to face south again. As you do that, your arms open to the sides with the forearms canted slightly forwards, at about a 45-degree angle in the front-back plane. Your hands will reach about your head height. Don't go nuts with this; no motion should ever be extreme. In particular, don't stretch your arms out straight; keep your forearms at a bit more than 90 degrees open with respect to the upper arms.

While doing that arm thing, your left foot had to pivot on the heel so your toes face directly forward. This means you had to remove all weight from the left foot, so it's a Cat-Step opportunity.

When the weight has been removed from the left foot, and after you've pivoted it into the correct final position, RAISE it, TOUCH down with the full sole, REST, and RELAX. Feel the SURGE.

Then you will circle your arms to the sides and down and your hands will cross at the wrists down below your abdomen, right arm on the inside. Shift all weight to your left foot (LOAD) as you pivot on your toe to bring your right heel inward. If you weren't doing any Cat-Step protocol training, you'd then raise your hands together in front of your body and begin to shift 50% of your body weight into the right foot, thus returning to the *Yubeishi* (Preparation Pose 1) form for your lower body.

In that case your arms would rise to cross just below your face as you shift weight to 50-50. You'd then lower them as your palms rotate outward to your sides, re-settling into full Preparation Pose 1.

However, even this little foot situation is a chance to introduce yet another Cat-Step. So after the right foot's toe pivot, when your right foot is weightless and positioned straight toward the front, RAISE it, TOUCH the full sole, REST it, RELAX it fully (leg weight only), and feel the SURGE. This SURGE, coming after all that prior work and coupled with a relatively easy overall pose (from the physical/mechanical point of view) will be one of the strongest you'll feel in the entire form practice.

If you're concluding your form practice here, you'd finish by bringing your feet together, back into Infinite Pose 0. The details are described for the identical final pose at the end of the full form, below.

Section 2

18 抱虎歸山 (bào hǔ guī shān)
Embrace tiger, return to mountain
(Northwest)

This pose creates a challenge right at the start – the big step to the right rear corner to get into it. We saw a fairly big step earlier for getting into Single Whip. But this step requires that your feet open significantly wider than 90 degrees. So if the Single Whip step-in was "wide angle", then this one should be called 'fish eye'. This is the first of *five* such super-wide 'fish eye' steps in the form.

You need to have a very strong supporting left leg, and at the same time a very loose and open right hip and thigh to achieve that TOUCH at the perfect right rear position, *without any weight*. The trick is to keep your upper body, especially your shoulders, entirely relaxed throughout the step and transition. Though your upper body must be entirely relaxed physically, you cannot let your hands energetically 'die'.

Apart from the physical challenge, this is a normal HEEL Cat-Step, and it delivers a great SURGE.

19 攔雀尾：捋 (lán què wěi：lǚ)
Grasp sparrow's tail: roll back

20 攔雀尾：擠 (lán què wěi：jǐ)
Grasp sparrow's tail: press

21 攔雀尾：按 (lán què wěi：àn)
Grasp sparrow's tail: push

22 斜單鞭 (xié dān biān)
Diagonal single whip

This entire set, from Pose 19 to Pose 22, is basically a duplicate of the first Grasp Sparrow Tail sequence from Section 1, ending with Single Whip. The only difference is the diagonal offset of the direction change into Single Whip. In Section 1, the axis went from West changing to East for the final Single Whip. Here, it is Northwest changing to Southeast. Otherwise, this sequence gives us the same chances to train our Cat-Step and Counter-Sink as the earlier sub-sequence in Section 1.

23 肘底捶 (zhǒu dǐ chuí)
Fist under elbow
(East)

Going from previous Single Whip to this pose gives you the chance to do two separate flat-footed (SOLE) Cat-Steps, first with your left foot, then with the right. The pose itself is another back-weighted 100/0 pose, right leg supporting, which gives you the option of doing your Counter-Sink on the left heel, with either HEEL TOUCH mode or HEEL REST mode (on the left heel).

24 倒攆猴 (dào niǎn hóu)
Step back repulse monkey
East

Now we come to one of the supremely powerful poses/sub-sequences in the entire form. You can really wring some serious internal training out of this subset. It has everything.

The minimal rep count for this would be three instances of the pose, but you can do any odd number of reps, as long as you have floor space going backward. There are a few little physical gotcha's. For example, in many other styles of Tai Chi Repulse Monkey, the feet splay outward in a duck-walk pattern on each backward step. In the ZMQ37, both feet are always keep train-rail straight on every back step. Learning to do this will engage your mind, and therefore your energy, to the utmost. So don't be lazy, check that your feet are lined up straight forward at the finish of every rep.

The first thing Repulse Monkey offers is the best chance for the Stationary Cat-Step to be found anywhere in the form. The narrow pose gives just the right balance and shape to get the most from the Stationary version of the Cat-Step. So, even though it isn't "necessary" to RAISE your front foot, every time you settle into the Repulse Monkey back-weighted stance, you'd be well-advised to RAISE your front foot in place, then TOUCH with the SOLE only, then REST on the sole, then RELAX and you'll feel a fantastic SURGE.

Then, because you are still in your Repulse Monkey stance (as the above Stationary Cat-Step didn't take you anywhere or change anything) you do your Counter-Sink to the normal silent count of 7.

In this Counter-Sink you'll feel the energy vibrating through you like nobody's business. Your arms will stream with some kind of ionized plasma feeling to your "fingerpaint" hands. In addition, you'll feel that your entire back (not just the spinal channel) has become thickly charged with slabs of internal power. That's probably why this is one of only two poses that Prof. Zheng was ever reported to have witnessed his own teacher, Yang Chengfu, practicing (the other was Single Whip).

The Counter-Sink in Repulse Monkey will bring home to you why in the Tai Chi classics it is written:

氣貼於背也
The qi adheres to the back

It's an incredibly strong and obvious back activation mechanism, what I call *backtivation*. Once you've felt it and can control it, you can directly channel this back energy up through your arms and out to your hands.

But the Repulse Monkey doesn't stop there, you have another chance to do a type of Cat-Step, the REAR Cat-Step to transition to the next (other side) rep. For this, step straight back with your foot RAISED but prepared to TOUCH with the toe/front of your foot. Feel that your ankle is relaxed and set properly so that when you drop down the entire foot, your toes won't be splayed out in a duck walk, but will be aligned train-rail straight along the main pose axis (toes point straight East at all times). Then, TOUCH your entire sole in the back.

This will be a bit tricky to learn to do. It's natural to begin to transfer body weight early on a REAR Cat-Step, but don't do that. Bend your supporting knee a bit more and sit as low as necessary to allow for a pure TOUCH with the toe/front of the stepping. Then, REST the foot on its toe/front. Now here's another challenge: you must transition from the toe/front REST to a full sole REST, but without adding any body weight yet.

That can be tricky but the solution is the same – try to sit a bit lower on your support leg to allow for this. Then, RELAX the entire rear -stepping leg. This will feel different from the RELAX stage of most of what's gone before. Most particularly, you need to relax the *back of your thigh* and *butt*. As you do so, you'll feel a wonderful SURGE. Then you can continue with the normal LOAD of the stepping leg and into the next side's Repulse Monkey.

25 斜飛勢 (xié fēi shì)
Diagonal flying
(Southwest)

After the final Repulse Monkey (which must end with a left-weighted rep), you encounter the transition into Diagonal Flying, which requires the second of the ZMQ form's five very wide-angle "fish eye" steps. Keep the upper body, especially shoulder, completely relaxed as you attempt the weightless TOUCH on this Cat-Step.

These "fish eye" super-wide steps give you a chance to push to the absolute limit your ability to TOUCH without any weight. At first, you may find that it's not possible for you to do the pure weightless TOUCH with your foot correctly positioned, contacting the heel only. In that case, just work toward it slowly by initially touching the heel with some additional weight, closer to the REST condition. Over time, try to back off all of that extra weight.

26 雲手 (yún shǒu)
Cloud hands
(South)

This is the second, after Repulse Monkey, of the truly fantastic *sub-sequences* of the ZMQ37 form. Like Repulse Monkey, it can be practiced in isolation. It can also be practiced in a stationary position, so you never run out of room as you will if you do the side-stepping (moving) version embedded in the form. Any way you practice it, it's truly a high octane engine of internal power.

Those who've read my earlier book *Peng* will recall that there I described the stationary version of Cloud Hands as an isolated drill. Here, I'll present the full version, which can be practiced in isolation or as part of the form. If it's done as part of the form, you should do at least three reps, or any odd number, to facilitate the transition to the ending pose, another Single Whip.

In Cloud Hands we can practice an interesting SIDE stepping version of the Cat-Step on every rep, and also a unique variant of the

Counter-Sink. The Cat-Step will be toward the left side, traveling eastward each time. The right foot steps about a shoulder-width or so distance toward the left foot. When the left foot steps leftward away from the right foot, it's a larger step, up to two shoulder-width lengths.

Every time you step, of course you must RAISE your foot, then you TOUCH down the entire SOLE, then REST on the sole (no body weight yet), then relax the entire leg, feel the SURGE (one of the best in the entire ZMQ). For some reason, in Cloud Hands it's very easy to mistakenly begin to elide or short-change the TOUCH stage. Unlike the "fish eye" steps, there is no physical challenge in the Cloud Hands TOUCH at all, in fact, this is probably the easiest TOUCH stage in the entire form. You're only stepping a shoulder width or so to the side every time.

But maybe just because it seems so easy, people get careless. Before you know it, the TOUCH has merged in with the REST, and eventually it's lost altogether. Don't let that happen! *If you skip the TOUCH you've lost the SURGE.*

After a full and proper sideward Cat-Step, you can begin to LOAD the stepping foot. After concluding the LOAD, which is the transition to the new weight-bearing leg, and which involves both a sideways-going weight shift and a turning of the waist toward the substantial (weighted) direction, you can do the Counter-Sink.

The Counter-Sink for Cloud Hands is unique. It involves lowering not only your body (by slightly relaxing the legs in small increments) but at the same time, you *lower your top arm* in concert with the overall body lowering, while *your lower arm rises.* All together. This arm exchange (upper arm drops on the outside, lower arm rises on the inside) must be performed anyway, even in the vanilla

103

version of the form (without Counter-Sink). But here, we do that arm exchange in tandem with the 7-count Counter-Sink motion, for a huge whole-body crystallization charge.

The key energetic aspect is to mentally engage your *rising* arm as active. The rising arm is the one really doing something. Let the lowering arm drop by itself, with a feeling as though it's merely dropping naturally along with your whole body's Counter-Sink.

27 單鞭 (dān biān)
Single Whip
(East)

This is another instance of Single Whip. Do the HEEL version of the Cat-Step, feel the SURGE, and do your Counter-Sink.

28 蛇身下勢 (shé shēn xià shì)
Snake Creeps Down
(East)

This is an athletically challenging pose. You must try to maintain the principle of Body Upright, but the lower you drop your body the harder that becomes. Try to keep your upper body and torso relaxed as you drop. The best way to approach it is to check your arms and shoulders for full relaxation before starting the drop, then during the actual lowering, keep your *legs* fully charged with your mind, from inguinal crease to the soles of your feet.

For this pose, the normal drop into the full (lowest) stage of the pose itself will automatically serve as the slow Counter-Sink, so you don't need to add any additional Counter-Sink. Once you're down there, you can push your left hand outward along the inside seam of your left leg pants and then begin to rise up on your left leg for the next (1 -legged) pose. This pose compresses the torso in a natural, relaxed way, and sets you up to feel a *gigantic* energy charge in the following two poses.

29 金雞獨立 (jīn jī dú lì)
Golden Rooster Single Leg
left and right versions
(East)

These poses allow you to check for total relaxation of your lower legs. That sets you up to do better RAISE stages of all subsequent Cat -Steps. So when you perform the Counter-Sink in this 1-legged pose, really try to let go of any tension in the toes, foot, ankle and calf of the RAISED leg. It may be challenging to lower very much when standing on a single leg, but it gives a great energy *crystallization*, so keep working on it.

The transition from the 1st of these (right leg raised) to the second (left leg raised) involves a side-rear Cat-Step. For the transition out of the first, you do a side-rear full SOLE TOUCH to the Southwest corner with your right foot. For the transition out of the second, you do a side-rear SOLE TOUCH to the Northwest corner with your left foot. Follow these SOLE TOUCH moves with the back version of REST, RELAX, and feel the SURGE in both cases. You'll find that these REAR Cat-Steps, if done precisely and consciously, will produce the biggest SURGES.

So far, I've covered two major sub-sequences which have especially powerful energetic effects and which can be practiced in isolation as uniform drills in their own right. They are Repulse Monkey and Cloud Hands. This Rooster pose can become the third such *super -sequence*, if you're willing to work it that way.

If you are too hide-bound, you won't be able to get your mind past the fact that this pose occurs only twice in the official version of the form. But once you begin to feel the total blow-out energy effects of doing it twice (particularly in charging your arms), you'll realize that you could just keep stepping backwards and perform this pose a total of any number of even reps. So it can work for you just like Repulse Monkey or Cloud Hands (except that they are done for an odd number of reps). The energetic charging effect of doing this for multiple reps (with Cat-Step and Counter-Sink each time of course) is mind-blowing.

30 分腳 (fēn jiǎo)
Separate Leg

This is one of the FREE leg poses covered in the *Peng* book (along with Golden Rooster). In the kicking shape, keep your thigh parallel to the floor, in other words, extended horizontally. Your foot is extended but must remain totally relaxed. Think of it as Beautiful Lady's Foot. Lower into your Counter-Sink as best you can. Keep your mental awareness in your two hands *yin mian* ('fingerpaint' hands) and the soles of both feet as you do so.

In transitioning after both of these kicks, you will do a sideward REAR Cat-Step, with the TOUCH on the full SOLE. Your foot will be positioned diagonally with toes out at 45 degrees. Since it's a REAR step it's a bit challenging, but squeeze all the energy you can from it. The key as always is to do a high-quality weightless TOUCH, and then do a full RELAX of those unfamiliar leg muscle engagements: back of thigh and butt. Feel the SURGE before moving into the next pose.

31 轉身蹬腳 (zhuǎn shēn dèng jiǎo)
Turn body heel kick

This pose offers a physical challenge of balance and control. You need to rotate about 180 degrees on your right heel, and then thrust out the left heel in a kind of push kick, using the full sole of the left foot. As you turn, you need to keep your arms really relaxed or you'll over-balance. This move isn't absolutely crucial for energy development, so if you have too much trouble with it, just skip it and move on to the next pose. But it's kind of fun once you've mastered it.

When you've got the kick fully extended, keep your leg out there, horizontally, for a full 7-tic Counter-Sink. Again, your mind is in the soles of both feet (one of which is raised, but no matter) and the palms/fingers of both hands.

To move on to the next pose, retract the kicking foot fully, then gently extend it again into a left side Cat-Step RAISE, HEEL TOUCH, etc. You'll be rewarded with a great SURGE at the end of that, because all the preceding kicking really charges up your entire lower body.

32 左右摟膝拗步 (zuǒ yòu lōu xī ào bù)
Left and right brush knee and twist step
(West)

From the preceding kick, you'll do yet another Brush Knee, which we've already covered. The transition between the left Brush Knee and the following right Brush Knee gives us a chance to first sit back on the right leg, do a Stationary Cat-Step (SOLE TOUCH) with the left leg, then LOAD the left leg and do a forward-stepping Cat-Step with the right foot, HEEL TOUCH. Feel the SURGE. Remember as before – it is Brush Knee, not Brush Thigh or Brush Waist. Keep body upright but really try to brush your palm across the front of your bent front knee.

33 進步栽捶 (jìn bù zāi chuí)
Advance plant punch
(West)

Figure 33: Heel Kick: apply the Counter-Sink as always. The distance of physical lowering is only 2 or 3 inches. The purpose is strictly to feel crystallization of internal energy.

This is the infamous low punch, which seems to violate our principle of *Body Upright.* What the hell - sometimes you gotta break the rules. This pose makes explicit what I've said all along, in all my books – *if you're relaxed, the other principles don't really matter.* (In fact, if you regard Tai Chi as a combat art, how *could* they possibly matter? You can't pre-stipulate that in a real fight on real terrain you will always and only remain in some particular prissy little posture or shape. The principles are just training wheels to help you get started feeling the energy from the form practice.)

We treat this pose like any other. Cat-Step into it with your left foot forward, then gently fold your upper body straight forward. Keep your butt aligned to the pose vector, not canted out to one side or the other – you'll need to be pretty relaxed in your torso to avoid that happening. The (right) punching forearm is parallel to the floor. There's also an alternate where the punch is slightly downward angled rather than parallel.

Keep your front knee directly above your front (left) toe, as always in front-weighted poses. Then do your Counter-Sink as always.

34 攔雀尾：右掤 (lán què wěi：yòu péng)
Grasp sparrow tail: ward-off (right)
(All West)

35 攔雀尾：捋 (lán què wěi：lǚ)
Grasp sparrow's tail: roll back

36 攔雀尾：擠 (lán què wěi：jǐ)
Grasp sparrow's tail: press

37 攔雀尾：按 (lán què wěi：àn)
Grasp sparrow's tail: push

38 單鞭 (dān biān)
Single whip
(East)

These are all duplicate poses. Work them hard for SURGE and Crystallization.

39 玉女穿梭（四） yù nǚ chuān suō
Fair lady weaving
(Southwest)

40 玉女穿梭（四） yù nǚ chuānsuō
Fair lady weaving
(Northeast)

41 玉女穿梭（四） yù nǚ chuānsuō
Fair lady weaving
(Northwest)

42 玉女穿梭（四） yù nǚ chuān suō
Fair lady weaving
(Southeast)

As you can infer from the directional indications above, there are *two* instances of very wide-angle steps in this mini-set of four basically identical poses. These two big steps are numbers three and four on the list of five total "fish eye" super wide-angle steps in the form. The challenge in each case is to perform a weightless TOUCH with the HEEL alone, so that you get a good SURGE. This may take weeks or months to master, but the more you relax your upper body and hip area as you step, the easier it will become.

The step after the last of these, into the next pose below, is the 5th and final super wide-angle "fish eye" step in the form. The same considerations of learning to step that far with a weightless HEEL TOUCH all apply.

43 攔雀尾：左掤 (lán què wěi：zuǒ péng)
Grasp sparrow's tail: ward-off (left)
(All West)

44 攔雀尾：右掤 (lán què wěi：yòu péng)
Grasp sparrow's tail: ward-off (right)

45 攔雀尾：捋 (lán què wěi：lǚ)
Grasp sparrow's tail: roll back

46 攔雀尾：擠 (lán què wěi：jǐ)
Grasp sparrow's tail: press

47 攔雀尾：按 (lán què wěi：àn)
Grasp the sparrow's tail: push

48 單鞭 (dān biān)
Single whip
(East)

49 蛇身下勢 (shé shēn xià shì)
Snake creeps down
(East)

All these poses have been covered previously.

50 上步七星 (shàng bù qī xīng)
Rise up to Seven Stars
(East)

After the previous Snake Creeps Down, you come up to this back-weighted pose. For this, as with all back-weighted poses where the front foot just touches the ground, you have your choice in the Cat-Step that brings your front foot into position, and in the subsequent Counter-Sink.

You can either end your Cat-Step with just a pure TOUCH alone, with no additional leg weight supported by the floor at all, or you can do your toe TOUCH followed by a REST of the leg weight into the floor (no body weight). Either way, try to relax the leg overall as much as possible.

Either option can give you a good surge here, but generally you'll feel the most charge with the TOUCH/REST option.

51 退步跨虎 (tuì bù kuà hǔ)
Step back and ride tiger
(East)

From the previous pose, you do a REAR Cat-Step, using the whole -foot (SOLE TOUCH) type, stepping to the Southwest. The resulting back-weighted pose, Ride Tiger, may give you the greatest *crystallization* of any move in this entire form. In the Repulse Monkey segment I talked about *backtivation* - the smearing of pure energy all over the back – muscles, spinal cord, skin - everything. That's the Tai Chi Classic principle: 氣貼於背 (*the energy adheres to the back*).

During the Counter-Sink, or frankly even *without* the Counter-Sink, this pose lights up your *back* like nothing else. It's the nature and structure of this pose to cause that training effect. So you may want to hold or Counter-Sink this pose longer than you would other poses.

Since it's one of the 100/0 back-weighted poses, you again have your choice of applying your front foot as only a TOUCH, or as a TOUCH followed by REST.

52 轉身擺蓮 (zhuǎn shēn bǎi lián)
Turn body and swing over lotus
(East)

This pose is an arm-swinging circular twirl, facing east at the beginning and end. You must relax your arms and the free leg completely in order to keep your balance and not over or under turn. It's a good quasi-physical challenge to your relaxation and control.

At the beginning your left foot is the free/unweighted foot, and you twirl on your right/rear foot. But as you finish, the weight switches completely to your left, so that the right becomes free for the subsequent crescent kick. For this twirl and the following kick, you don't need to bother with the Counter-Sink protocol.

The kick itself is interesting as it further activates your *da ling* point (an energy hot spot in the mid/upper spine, extensively discussed in my other book, *Juice*). To intensify that effect, you could remain in place supported by your left leg, and continuously repeat the relaxed crescent (Lotus) kick with your right leg. This mode is performed in a free video on my YouTube channel *livewireqi*, titled 'JUICE *Accelerant: Crescent Kick*')

Try to bring your foot to your hands rather than aggressively leaning forward to touch your kicking foot. The leg is not locked but not excessively bent either; it should feel 'bent seeking straightness'. (If you do a series of kicks in place like this, you can perform the Counter-Sink after each repetition of the kick, with your right knee held up.)

When done with kicking, you step outward with the right foot to the Southwest corner in a regular HEEL TOUCH Cat-Step, no weight.

53 彎弓射虎 (wān gōng shè hǔ)
Bend bow shoot tiger
(Southeast)

This pose is a standard front-weighted 70/30 (or 80/20) thing. Both your hands are in fists here. Do your Counter-Sink as always, but instead of mentally engaging the palms and inner fingers (*yin mian*), here you have a chance again to do the *my hands felt just like two balloons* idea (song lyric mentioned earlier).

54 進步搬攔捶 (jìn bù bān lán chuí)
Advance, deflect, parry and punch
(East)

55 如封似閉 (rú fēng sì bì)
Apparent closing
(East)

56 十字手 (shí zì shǒu)
Cross hands
(South)

All these are duplicates of poses discussed earlier at the end of Section 1.

57 合太極 (hé tài jí)
Conclude tai chi
(South)

I will discuss this concluding pose in connection with the *Tai Chi Bread Sandwich* (compressed training method) in the next section.

Figure 34: Low Punch "Let the feather weigh you down"

Figure 35: Step Back Ride Tiger with Counter-Sink protocol. You'll really feel the *qi* adhering to your back.

Figure 36: Lotus Kick: Begin with knee raised; arms and fingers gently extended.

Figure 37: Begin kick with foot outside your left fingertips., then brush them going rightward.

Figure 38: Lotus Kick: Sweep foot sideward, across and between hands.

Figure 39: Lotus Kick: sweep foot all the way across and outside of right fingers.

Figure 40: Lotus Kick: Return to start position for another kick rep, or Cat-Step into Bend Bow Shoot Tiger.

Bread Sandwich Tai Chi

You can practice the key internal conditioning methods of this book without performing, or even knowing, any of the form.

It's always better to do more. Do the entire form whenever you can. But here's a simple procedure that encompasses all the important elements and principles, which can be done any place, any time.

1. Open with 2 Cat-Steps

2. Counter-Sink in *Yubeishi*

3. Close with 2 Cat-Steps

All that can be done in less than five minutes in a space the size of a bath mat. Since it's only the opening and closing pose, without any 'form' in between, I call it *Bread Sandwich Tai Chi.*

The 1st phase and 2nd phases are exactly as specified for the transition from Pose 0 (*Unlimited*) to Pose 1 (*Preparation*). That covers your first two Cat-Steps and the Counter-Sink.

Then you jump directly to the finish, as though you had done the entire form. To do that, you shift all weight to your left leg. RAISE the right foot a few centimeters and open the toes to about 30 degrees. Then, your right foot will SOLE TOUCH (no weight at all), then SOLE REST, then RELAX, then you'll feel the SURGE.

This simple standing pose gives one of the best SURGES, if you bend your knees to add some mass to the REST phase (leg weight only). After feeling that SURGE, LOAD all weight into your right leg. Now RAISE your left foot, bring it over sideways so your left heel touches your right heel, but your left toe angles outward at 30 degrees (the same outward angles the feet had begun with, at the starting Unlimited pose). Then you TOUCH SOLE, REST SOLE, RELAX, and feel the final SURGE, just as with the right foot.

Advanced Work

What is this power flowing
In our bodies like fire?
What is it?

That power is like hot iron,
Ready to pour.

Choose the mold,
and the power will scorch it.

- Mahabharata

If you have understood and felt the basic work with the two proto-cols, you can play with these more advanced versions. Don't bother with these until you've actually felt what I've described in the basic sections. The basics are more than sufficient to blast your internal power straight up to the sky. Conversely, if you rush into these ad-vanced versions, you might get frustrated and quit the whole pro-gram in disgust. So, take it slow and easy.

Cat-Step Protocol/CYCLING:

So far, I've presented the Cat-Step SURGE as a one-time thing. You Cat-Step, you feel the SURGE, and you LOAD into the next pose. In advanced mode, you find that it's possible to generate the SURGE in *multiple pulses*, for as long as you want. After the first SURGE, once the power has reached your hands, instead of going into LOAD, maintain the same physical configuration (typically with one leg out in front, to the side, or in back, with only that leg's weight supported on the floor, in REST/RELAX mode). Then, put your mind into your *strong* foot, the *supporting* foot. As you do so, you'll feel a secondary SURGE coming up from *both* feet. Once that reaches the hands (only a half second or so), you can repeat as many times as you want, under purely mental control.

Counter-Sink Protocol/PACKING:

The Counter-Sink has been described so far as requiring mental focus on four surfaces: the *yin mian* (陰面; inner surfaces) of both hands, and the soles of your feet (no special *yong quan* points or *three nails* or anything exotic is necessary, just the full flat surfaces there). That's already a fair amount of real estate to focus on, a lot of mental overhead for a beginner. But if you've felt the *crystallization* whole-body energy lattice, you can consider a further turn of the screw. One more focus point can be added: the *dantian*.

You would then keep your mental awareness on the original four surfaces, and also on the *dantian*. For best effect, you conceive of the *dantian* as a spot that isn't deep *inside* your lower abdomen as normally described, but on the *surface* of your lower belly. Imagine a small coin such as a dime or nickel has been taped to the outer skin of your lower belly, a couple inches or so below your navel, right where it begins to curve inward toward the pubic bone.

That's your focus spot. This mental target gives a better energetic result in the Counter-Sink than the inner *dantian* location usually advised, which is more difficult to feel. In the long run it all comes

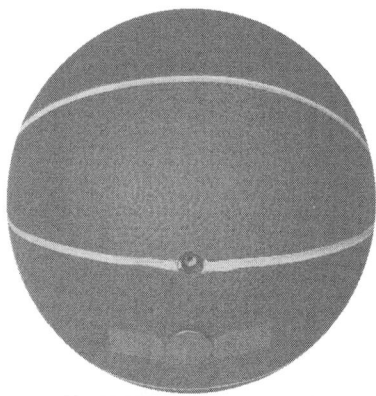

Figure 41: *Dantian* should be visualized as a coin placed on the curved *surface* of the lower belly.

down to the same thing, a full inner activation of the entire *qi hai* (氣海) lower belly area.

Although the ZMQ37 Tai Chi system is complete in itself, I've noticed over the years that too many people have trouble feeling into the *dantian* directly. It seems to be a mentally and energetically opaque area for most students and even a number of teachers. But you need to feel your *dantian* pulsing and vibrating with constant power for real, or all this will remain merely ossified Eastern philosophy. Which it isn't, it's a daily human reality.

To help a beginner with this, I sometimes borrow a drill from Xingyiquan (another Chinese internal martial art). This drill is not native to Tai Chi, much less to the ZMQ37 system. So if you're concerned about pollution or pristine purity, please skip this section. And even if you provisionally adopt it, it's only useful in Tai Chi as a training wheel thing. Play with it until you get the idea and the right feeling, then drop it. Continue to work on the concept and feeling within your Tai Chi Counter-Sink protocol.

This drill is depicted on my Youtube channel (*livewireqi*) with a basic Xingyi posture in the short training clip titled *Infinite Power Poles #4*. For learning to locate and feel into the *dantian* for Tai Chi, you can use any Tai Chi pose instead, such as Repulse Monkey (introduced in the *Peng* book).

Figure 42: Bracing the far end against a corner; gently maintain the *lightest possible* pressure on the near end at your *dantian* spot, without letting the pole drop away. Keep a mental goal of further lightening the staff pressure against abdomen, to the very instant of feeling it drop away. (Illustration is performed with a Xingyi pose, but you can substitute any Tai Chi pose)

Stand in one of the back-weighted Tai Chi poses, such as Repulse Monkey (later you can use any other pose). Brace one end of the staff against a corner or base of a wall. Set the other end gently at the *dantian* point as indicated by the coin visualization. The pole doesn't rest 'on' your belly, it is very lightly and gently pressing 'against' your belly. But do not press yourself *into* the pole, rather, without moving your feet, try to draw your *dantian away* from the pole.

This would make the pole drop, but – *don't allow the pole to drop or move.* It's one of these paradoxical impossible tasks. That's where power arises, at the border of the impossible. Work one side for a few minutes and then change sides. Keep subtly trying to draw your *dantian* away from the pole, yet without ever losing contact or allowing the end of the pole to slip down even slightly.

This staff drill is merely an auxiliary practice, not part of the Tai Chi form. But once you've learned to feel the *dantian*, you can apply your experience to your Tai Chi form practice. Lower in Counter-Sink with your mind engaged now at all *five* locations (feet and hands, as before, and now *dantian*). This advanced mode has a strange but fascinating *packing* effect on your torso. Your entire torso, front, sides and back, will feel like a large, strong barrel of something thick and powerful. Doesn't matter whether you are physically fat or fit because this is an energetic effect.

But don't do this before you have felt and controlled the full state of feet-to-hands *crystallization*. If you try this prematurely, your energy will tend to get kind of stuck in a partial zone. The ultimate goal of this work is always consistent: *feet to fingers!*

Cestus Protocol/EDGING:

I haven't mentioned the *cestus* concept yet in this book, because it's borrowed over from my book *Radical Xingyi Energetics*. There, I define the *cestus* region as your forearm, wrist, and all of your hand or fist. It's the body area covered by the ancient gladiator arm protection gear known as the *cestus* glove –a weapon of their times.

It's a strangely useful concept for energy work, and not only in Xingyi. It aligns perfectly with the ZMQ Beautiful Lady's Hand shape – the idea of a continuous surface from forearm to hand, across the flat back wrist. No bend in the wrists. This shape is invariant throughout the whole ZMQ form, except for the Commencement wrist bends and Single Whip's hook-hand.

I've talked about stepping in *transitions* (the Cat-Step) and sinking in *poses* (the Counter-Sink). But I haven't said anything about your upper body and arms during the actual moves of Tai Chi. After all, once you begin to LOAD following every Cat-Step, before you achieve the final static form of the pose which is your launchpad for the Counter -Sink, you have to pass through a stage where you form your arms and upper body into the correct shape for the pose.

We can use this additional phase of the practice to augment our energy experience. It's very simple: just keep your mind at the outer edge of both forearms, extending all the way to the outer edge of your hand and pinky finger, as you move your arms and do the strike or whatever the posture calls for. That is mainly the bony ridge of the ulna bone, but mentally include the meat of the inside and lower forearm also.

You'll feel that the *physical line* of the forearm and wrist, as required by the Beautiful Lady's Hand principle, coheres perfectly with the *energetic line* that bursts along the edge of the *cestus* region as defined in the Xingyi material. *Don't tense up at all when doing this.* It's purely a question of mental awareness in movement. The mental awareness alone will draw the power to the indicated area.

This does not conflict with or overlap on the Cat-Step (your arms don't move during the Cat-Step, thus you can concentrate on the Cat-Step lower-body work). Nor does it conflict with the Counter-Sink, because you don't begin the Counter-Sink until you have fully formed the pose and all other movement has ceased. The Edging practice is only for that gray zone that I've left undefined so far, which is the very thing that most Tai Chi students and teachers mainly focus on – the arm dynamics. The reason most people focus on those is that they are fun and showy.

But in this system they're secondary. After you've understood the other two protocols, you can add this in. If added in at that point in your development, the EDGING practice is a very powerful supplement to your internal regimen.

Counter-Sink Protocol/PINNING:

Pinning is the most advanced mode of Counter-Sink work and should only be attempted after you've gotten a solid experience with the 4-surfaces version and then begun to integrate the *dantian* in 5-surfaces PACKING mode, as described above.

Once you've really got the energy running in those basic modes, you'll realize that you only need the *dantian* in your Counter-Sinking to get the full effect. The emphasis on feet and hands in the earlier stage was to clear the path and make sure you don't leave any limb energetically dead and unconnected.

In PINNING, you do the 7-count Counter-Sink as before, and you concentrate mainly on the *dantian* as you do so. But there's one additional wrinkle: *you create the feeling that your hands and arms are 'pinned' in place*, at whatever configuration and level the pose calls for. In other words, *your hands and arms don't participate* in the Counter-Sink lowering.

After assuming the pose, you lower your torso by bending your legs as usual, but as you do so, you imagine that your arms are pinned in place. So they don't lower nor do they participate in the

Figure 43: Do the Counter-Sink without allowing your arms to lower, holding them in full configuration, and as though they were supported and restrained in place - PINNED

'drawdown'. Your arms remain in the full and correct configuration called for by the pose.

This works because the lowering isn't physically extreme. If it were, PINNING the hands in place while lowering would wind up with you in a severely distorted final shape. But with the physically minimal lowering of a very small distance, an outside observer would barely be able to detect any difference.

PINNING is intimately tied to relaxation. You want to generate a feeling that you are deliberately creating a larger and larger *gap* between your *dantian* and your hands. Feel that without moving your hands, you're infinitely expanding the space between your hands and your *dantian*. The only way to get the space you'll need for that is to relax your entire upper body. *If your upper body isn't relaxed, your torso won't be able to sink independently* of your arms. If you aren't relaxed, your tightly linked arms will be dragged down along with your torso in the Counter-Sink.

This implies that while we envision our arms as invariant, it's really the forearms and hands that are PINNED, because there must be some degree of movement in the relaxed elbows and shoulders that allows your torso to sink while your *cestus* zones and hands are held in place. As always with the Counter-Sink, it's not a large distance of drop, it's minimal and subtle.

The composite photo illustrating the Counter-Sink for the pose Heel Kick (in the chapter *Pose Notes*) shows only the basic mode of Counter-Sink, which is visually more obvious. If I'd been performing the PINNING Counter-Sink in that pose, my hands (and foot) would have remained in place as my supporting leg bent while my torso lowered.

You'll feel the kinship of PINNING to the Xingyi *dantian* pole drill described above. They are both working in a minimal intimate space to create a powerful and distinct effect of *dantian* engagement. It's an impetus to retract, withdraw and sink the *dantian*, and yet to keep it in energetic relation to something else (the pole or your hands) that generates the huge surges of *peng* power that will eventually pulse in your *dantian* area night and day, 24/7.

This is not akin to the imaginary, hyper-dimensional cables, springs, ropes, walls, pulleys, ratchets, and other mental gear used in Yi Quan *zhan zhuang* imagery. This is much simpler – merely keep your hands (and the raised foot in the kicks) at invariant height as the rest of your body lowers. This will tremendously amplify your energetic surges and states.

Cat-Step Protocol/GAPPING:

If you've practiced everything up to this point in this chapter, and you've really begun to understand the key feelings involved, you may be ready to try GAPPING. Though it sounds simple, it's extremely powerful, but *only* if you've really worked deeply with the basic Cat-Step and Counter-Sink protocols, the PACKING variation, and the PINNING extension that follows on from that. Don't bother with GAPPING until you've got a solid grounding in those pre-requisites.

This is a simple extension to the RELAX (final phase of the Cat-Step, right before you LOAD body weight onto the stepping foot). All you need to do is remain a few extra seconds in the final REST/RELAX condition, and withdraw your *dantian* slightly. This will make no sense and be impossible for you if you haven't understood and accepted the "surface coin" idea of the *dantian*, so please review the previous sections and the illustration above before attempting this.

Just feel you are opening up a gap, a little extra distance between your stepping foot (by now it's flat on the floor, the very end of the Cat-Step) and your *dantian*. Your feet and arms don't move at all. Everything stays in place on the floor. Only your *dantian* withdraws very slightly, away from the foot.

Whereas PINNING is a sinking process (a version of the Counter-Sink) GAPPING is closer to being a slight *level* or *horizontal* movement of your *dantian* "away" from the lead/stepping foot. Open up a slight gap between them by using subtle *dantian* movement. I know - it sounds too simple, as radically powerful practices will.

WU BI ZHUANG (無臂樁) Armless Standing

Now we come full circle. After those more involved practices (but they're not all that complex, are they, really?) we return to take another look at plain vanilla *holding a pose*. But, as always, there's going to be a special twist.

This entirely depends on your prior work with all the other stuff I've already covered. If you jump straight to this, you'll get nothing. It'll be merely Yet Another Drill (YAD) gathering dust on your shelf. But if you phase it in after you've really begun to trigger the energies via the pre-requisite work, this will launch you beyond near-earth orbit – escape velocity.

Don't be fooled by how simple it looks. All my stuff appears a lot simpler than conventional Qi Gong, Zhan Zhuang, and Yi Quan. But it's ultimately more effective, because simplicity is more conducive to mental and physical relaxation.

The drill is drop-dead simple, just three easy steps. But before getting down to it, I emphasize that though your standing is *static*, this is an *active* drill. Although the work is 99% mental, the experience and result of it is not a visual image or mind concept. Rather, it's a tangible charge and surge in your body. You have to really feel the different charges at each stage. If you aren't palpably and tangibly feeling the power surges at every stage then either:

1. you're doing this drill wrong; or

2. you aren't ready for it yet.

In that case, back off to the earlier stuff in this section or to the basic protocols. You've wasted enough time in your Tai Chi practice life on drills that have become mindless wooden rote. Don't let this become just another. Once you get the knack of this, you'll realize that it has everything I described for ideal Tai Chi practice: Grounding, Relaxation, Extension, and Mindfulness.

Stage 1: Assume any of the 37 poses. It makes no difference which one. Choose your favorite. My teacher always said: If you attend a party with 37 people, you may not find everybody fascinating, but with that many people you can always find somebody cool to hang with. Get into that pose in *zhan zhuang* (static) mode. Form it as best you can according to all the principles – Relaxed, Upright, Waist straight, Beautiful Lady's Hand, and Weight correctly proportioned for that pose.

Stage 2: Imagine for a moment that your arms are GONE. I mean really gone, they have vanished, dropped off you, *poof* ... gone. You make no *physical* change to your pose whatsoever. You don't drop or droop your arms. It's purely mental. And it's only for a instant, not a long drawn out meditation thing. This is an *active* process. For a moment your whole body will be there, but you'll have no arms – like one of those damaged Roman or Greek statues. This will instantaneously charge up your body from the soles of your feet to the crown of your head.

Stage 3: Now instantly, bring your arms back. Of course, your posture has never physically changed at all. In the previous stage, your arms vanished because your mind abandoned them. Now you put your mind 100% back into your arms. VOOM! You'll feel the gigantic rush of energy into your arms, from shoulders to fingertips, followed by a whole-body smoothing out of the energy from feet to fingertips. Repeat Steps 2 and 3 as many times as desired (and once you first feel the power of this, you'll desire it more and more).

Figure 44: Wu Bi Zhuang - Make your arms 'disappear' (left); then mentally re
-engage them (right)

Zhang Zhuang/PINNED

This is the most powerful Tai Chi internal practice in this book. I always seem to be saying that, don't I? But that's true for each stage.
It's cumulative. Zhang Zhuang/PINNED incorporates almost everything else described in this book. The result is a slightly odd practice
that may feel awkward to some people, may scandalize others in its
apparent unorthodoxy, or may appear unacceptably elementary to
yet others. But if you can get past your hang-ups and apply everything you should have learned from this book to working it hard, it
really delivers the goods.

I'll call it ZZP for short. To perform ZZP, you must have understood
and practiced the basic *Zhang Zhuang* method described in the earlier book *Peng Root Power Rising*. If you got the idea of that, then ZZP
is a simple variation. For ZZP, you do the 'slump' as in basic ZZ, but
you *do not include your arms*. In other words, your arms remain exactly and perfectly positioned as they should be for the full pose.

In the basic ZZ, your arms lose their shape, you release the Fair
Lady's Hand, and let your hands and arms droop down with the rest

of the upper body. But in ZPP, your arms (the *cestus* zones of hands and forearms) stay fully shaped and also "pinned" in place. You only slump your head, neck, and torso. Then you 'refill' as with basic ZZ. Your arms haven't changed position, but they will inflate hugely with giant surges of energy from your feet, in multiple cycles over 30 seconds or so. Repeat as desired.

Figure 45: With basic *Zhang Zhuang* you allow your entire upper body, including arms and hands, to slightly slump or 'drawdown' and then 're-activate' back to the full and correct configuration for the pose

You can practice this with any named pose of the ZMQ37 set. In addition to the seven basic poses introduced in the *Peng* book, for a good *back-weighted* pose (0/100 or 20/80) that will seriously get

Figure 46: With Zhang Zhuang PINNED, you begin the Zhang Zhuang 'drawdown' (upper body slump) without allowing your arms to lower, holding them in the full configuration - PINNED as though they were supported and restrained in place. You then 'reactivate' your back, neck and head to the full and correct configuration for the pose

you feeling the augmented arm energy quickly and strongly, experiment with Pose 50: *Rise up to Seven Stars*.

When working ZZP with *front-weighted poses* (70/30 or 80/20 distribution), be sure that your front knee is well bent and precisely positioned directly over your front toe as you begin. To help insure that configuration, you may want to optionally perform the Counter -Sink immediately before doing the ZZP. Then take care to *maintain* your front knee well-bent, directly over the front toe as you re -activate. This is not an overall 'rising' exercise, because the lower

Figure 47: Contrast of initial 'drawdown' positions for basic ZZ (left) and ZZP (right). The figure on the left has included her arms and hands in the 'drawdown'. The figure on the right has her hands in the full and correct height and shape for the pose.

body remains in place, invariant. But you should feel as though *energetically* you are re-engaging from the single strong foot upward through torso, neck and head. Correct knee depth and placement in the front-weighted stances will greatly intensify how strongly this practice lights you up.

Counter-Sink Protocol/SUPER SURGE:

The Super Surge isn't something you *do*; it's something that *happens* to you as a result of doing all the other stuff.

One day, after a few months of practicing all the methods in this book, integrated with the ZMQ37 form, you'll be standing in a 70/30 pose. It will most likely be Single Whip or perhaps one of the 70/30 (front-weighted) stances in the *Grasp Sparrow Tail* sequence. Before you can even begin your Counter-Sink, a gigantic surge of energy will suddenly well upward from the soles of your feet.

The normal SURGE from the Cat-Step is already phenomenal, unbelievable really, but you will have got somewhat used to that. And the *crystallization* likewise is startling when you first feel it, but you will have learned by now to generate that at will and control it deftly at some point. No matter how far you've gotten with all that, your first Super Surge will take you by surprise.

Try not to let it freak you out, don't start flailing around with the random movements called *kriya* in the yogic tradition. If you give in to that temptation you'll always be an amateur, you'll never learn to control the energy fully. Just ride it, feel it, relax into it. Eventually it will die down, and you can continue your regular practice calmly. Over time this will happen more and more frequently, so get used to it.

Refund Policy

I've wanted to feel pleasure to the point of insanity. They call it getting high, because it's wanting to know that higher level, that godlike level. You want to touch the heavens, you want to feel glory and euphoria, but the trick is it takes work. You can't buy it, you can't get it on a street corner, you can't steal it or inject it or shove it up your ass, you have to earn it.

- Anthony Kiedis

Note: *If you've enjoyed this book and gotten something out of it, I'm not talking to you here. This is for haters only. But you may want to read this section anyway, as it makes a few teaching points. Do I seem a tad defensive? Hey – I'm supposed to be a* **martial artist**, *right? 'Defensive' comes with the territory!*

I'm not going to make it easy for you, but the possibility of a refund does exist. Pitch your complaint to me via email (you can easily find me on the web) and I'll take one of the following actions in response:

1. Deny your refund without explanation

2. Deny your refund with explanation

3. Donate your purchase price to *Doctors Without Borders* in your name

4. Refund your purchase price via PayPal

Number 4 is the least likely but it's possible. So let me back up a little here and give you some context.

To get your refund, sell me on one of the following, make me feel your pain:

1. You don't believe there's any such thing as *peng* energy surging from feet to hands, despite what the Classics specify.

2. You believe in the existence of the *peng* energy, but you already have it very strongly on your own, or from other teachings, in any case without these bogus methods.

3. You believe in the existence of the *peng* energy, though you haven't experienced it, but you don't believe these phony methods would ever get you there.

4. You believe in the existence of the *peng* energy, though you haven't experienced it, but you feel that plugging along with your existing training will get you to it just fine, without such stupid frippery (this book).

The bar is high for getting your refund. First, you need to convince me you even *read* the thing. That sounds like a joke, but you'd be surprised. One tool did a review of *Peng* in which he (initially, now deleted) claimed that I did not mention or explain the Five Main Training Principles (they're in this book too: *Relax, Body Upright,* etc.) But on examination, even a monkey could see that all five are in fact listed and explained in great depth over multiple pages in that book. The *Beautiful Lady's Hand* is illustrated with a close-up photo, *Turn Waist* is the subject of several specific specialized drills, *Relax* is hammered again and again, *Separate Weight* and discussion of Substantial/Insubstantial is almost the entire point of the book, discussed over many pages.

Then, if you can convince me you even read it, I need to know whether you *understood* it. Understanding is a shared responsibility between reader and author. So it's possible your misunderstanding of the method, despite my repeated, multiple explanations of the basic protocols in this book, their many dozens of specific applications to every single pose in the entire ZMQ37 form and so on, is my fault. It's possible that somehow I have failed to communicate how to do these, simple though they are. But we need to make certain that's *my* fault and not *yours*. Therefore, if you take the incomprehensibility line, you'll need to furnish written proof that your IQ is over 90 and that your reading level is above Grade 6. Otherwise I'll kick back the claim as your own deficiency.

Further, I need to know that you made a sincere effort to *apply* the practices over a decent interval. Look, I know that *life is short and art is long*. I'm not insisting on decades here. But one joker responded with a very hostile review of *Peng* within a *week or two* of its being listed for sale. That's definitely slipping lead in the gloves, and I won't tolerate it. You have to make some reasonable effort over some reasonable period.

If you can jump all the above hurdles, you may be a good candidate for a refund. But I must still feel from your petition that you're a sincere, rational, courteous, well-meaning person. If I don't feel it, you ain't getting it. This book cost you no more than the price of a movie ticket for *Transformers: Age of Extinction* or whatever garbage, plus maybe a medium popcorn and small Coke. You won't get a refund for disliking that kind of crap, and I'm not inclined to be any more sympathetic than your local Cineplex.

Regardless of how many decades you've practiced or taught Tai Chi, and regardless of how many full-contact fights you may have notched on your belt, you need to ask yourself two questions:

1. Before reading this book, had you been practicing, in every precise, specific detail exactly the Cat-Step protocol and Counter-Sink protocol, as presented here? Not just: *Yeah, I've heard about cat-step and sitting low...* No, I mean the precise specifics – had you been performing those in your daily practice?

2. Before reading this book and trying these specific protocols, had you strongly and consistently felt the *peng* energy SURGE from feet to fingers as described here, in every Tai Chi practice session?

If the answer to both is honestly and emphatically *yes*, then you probably are a good candidate for the straight refund.

Look. Maybe you got nothing from this book – no *understanding*, no training *ideas*, no *entertainment*, no *education* of any kind. Or perhaps you made a sincere effort with the method and you found it was too radically innovative and thus **TOO NEW**, too far from what your teacher has taught, or too remote from a book you've previously read and enjoyed, and that was so scary you couldn't even approach it.

Or possibly, conversely, you felt it's all **TOO OLD** and tired, just what's in the Classics already have, or what your teacher's already told you, and these special energy practices within the form add NOTHING to what you've already done as a matter of course, just by sitting low in your postures and relaxing (in that case, as Solazzo said, raising his glass to the Godfather: *Te salud, Don Corleone!*)

In both cases, I would reply that, yes, these ideas are absolutely embedded dead straight within the classical ZMQ framework, but the approach is innovative in that I bet you are not practicing precisely this way right now. Maybe you try to sit low in your poses, and step softly, but I'm offering you a much more precisely articulated framework and more approachable method for those generic ideals. And it really *works*, hands down.

So it's new in the sense that it's turning traditional ideas into a more precise method. But at the same time, it's absolutely rooted in the Tai Chi Classics. It's the famous Cat-Step and rooting/sinking principle of Tai Chi. Nothing radical about that. So I would call it innovative at the level of *detail*, but traditional at the level of *principle*. That's exactly what we need. Best of both worlds. Some people love to carp rather than just try it out and make it work.

Or, maybe you feel the method is **TOO SIMPLE**, that you could've just figured this out on your own, and anyway it's way too rudimentary to get you where you want to be as a Taoist immortal.

Or you may feel it's way **TOO COMPLEX**, such that you say to yourself: *Why do I need all these piddling little methods... I just do my form every day and I'm fine.*

To cover all these **TOO X** cases, I would say: *It's just right.* Too *simple*? You should be eagerly on the lookout for useful simplifications, as long as they work. When it comes to internal power training, a lot of people want to gild the lily and get into lots of unrealistically complex practices that few people can sustain over months and years.

Too *complex*? Well, many people are practicing the postures woodenly, without thinking and feeling deeper into it, without digging up the real purpose, which is to spark the palpable internal energy. So again I would say this approach is just as complicated as it needs to be, to get you feeling what you really came in the door for.

But if, after sincerely watching and practicing this method for at least two months, you honestly conclude it isn't for you, then send your Amazon proof of purchase information to the email in my blog, along with your note explaining which of the above cases applies to you. And if you seem like a decent, honest, intelligent person with no special agenda or ax to grind, it's possible – though not guaranteed – that I will cheerfully refund your big bucks layout, via PayPal. Because when all's said and done, I'm well aware that this level of intense and direct energy training simply isn't for everybody.

THE BIG PICTURE

The secret to making a great album is to get the fuck out of the studio before you're sick of all the songs.

- Kurt Cobain

The sentiment expressed by Cobain above is absolutely right on. And he took it farther than just the 'studio' - his whole life and death was an expression of that core idea. The one amazing exception to his accurate appraisal of things is Tai Chi.

I say *amazing* because after all, in ZMQ37 Tai Chi, no matter how many years you practice, you're always doing the same thing. Talk about Ground Hog Day! Just those same 37 moves, over and over, day in and day out.

And yet, if you take the radically energy-centric approach, you never get 'sick of all the songs'. That's because Tai Chi is not a string of *physical* moves and poses. It's a set of energetic experiences. Each pose is a unique little drug trip of ecstatic energy in a slightly different flavor or vector of motion or depth. And the same poses will trigger deeper and deeper energetic responses in you by the day, by the month, by the year.

Chuck Palahniuk has written: "*You realize that people take drugs because it's the only real personal adventure left to them in their time-constrained, law-and-order, property-lined world. It's only in drugs or death we'll see anything new.*"

Well, yes and no. Daily life probably has enough chills and thrills to suit most of us, just from the ongoing Samsaric grind. Not to mention, if people are all *that* bored, there's always extreme sports.

Nevertheless, we kind of get Chuck's point there. It sometimes seems that only *drugs* and *war* can make us feel alive. But before reaching for the needle or crack spoon, not to mention the guns and bombs, I wish people could look within. I still cling by my toenails to the stupid rosy fantasy that war need not be the only force that gives us meaning.

स्वदेहे जगतो वापि सूक्ष्मसूक्ष्मतराणि च

तत्त्वानि यानि निलयं ध्यात्वान्ते व्यज्यते परा

Experience the substance of the body
And the world
As made up of vibrating particles,
And these particles made up of
Even finer energies.
Drifting more deeply,
Feel into each pulse of energy
As it condenses from infinity
And dissolves back into it
Continuously.

- Sutra of the *Vijnana Bhairava Tantra*

BIBLIOGRAPHY

Best photographic reference for the ZMQ37 postures:

T'ai Chi Ch'uan:
A Simplified Method of Calisthenics for Health & Self Defense
Cheng Man-Ch'ing (author)
Blue Snake Books; 1993

Best video reference for the ZMQ37 postures:

Professor Cheng Man Ch'ing's Simplified T'ai chi Ch'uan (37 Postures)
Benjamin Pang Jeng Lo (1991)

Full explanation of the Tai Chi Classic Writings:

The Lectures with Benjamin Pang Jeng Lo - 4 DVD Set
Benjamin Pang Jeng Lo (author)
IRI Press; 2010

Sanskrit translations from:

The Radiance Sutras (Vijnana Bhairava Tantra)
Lorin Roche (translator);
Sounds True; 2014

吾何以知衆甫之狀哉以此

9716730R00089

Printed in Great Britain
by Amazon.co.uk, Ltd.,
Marston Gate.